Couples Communication Code

End the Cycle of Fights, Rebuild Trust and Talk Honestly Without Triggering Each Other for Conflict-Free Conversations, Deeper Connection and Lasting Love

George Munson

GL Digital Publishing LLC

Copyright © 2025 by George Munson

All rights reserved.

No portion of this book may be reproduced without written permission from the publisher or author except as permitted by U.S. copyright law.

This publication is designed to provide accurate and authoritative information regarding the subject matter covered. It is sold with the understanding that neither the author nor the publisher is engaged in rendering legal, investment, accounting, or other professional services.

While the publisher and author have used their best efforts in preparing this book, they make no representations or warranties with respect to the accuracy or completeness of the contents of this book and specifically disclaim any implied warranties of merchantability or fitness for a particular purpose. No warranty may be created or extended by sales representatives or written sales materials.

The advice and strategies contained herein may not be suitable for your situation. You should consult with a professional when appropriate. Neither the publisher nor the author shall be liable for any loss of profit or other commercial damages, including but not limited to special, incidental, consequential, personal, or other damages.

Neither the publisher nor the author claims responsibility for the persistence or accuracy of URLs for external or third-party Internet Websites referred to in this publication, and does not guarantee that any content on such Websites is, or will remain, accurate or appropriate.

COUPLES COMMUNICATION CODE

Designations used by companies to distinguish their products are often claimed as trademarks. All brand names and product names used in this book and on its cover are trade names, service marks, trademarks and registered trademarks of their respective owners. The publishers and the book are not associated with any product or vendor mentioned in this book. None of the companies referenced within the book have endorsed the book.

First Edition 2025

Contents

Introduction

1. Understand the Fundamentals of Communication
    - The Art of Empathy in Conversations
    - Build Emotional Intelligence Together
    - Active Listening Goes Beyond Just Hearing
    - Identify and Bridge Empathy Gaps
    - The Science of Emotional Connection

2. Recognize and Break Negative Communication Patterns
    - Recognize High-Frequency Patterns of Frustration
    - Understand Your Partner's Emotional Triggers
    - How to Break the Blame Loop
    - Overcome Communication Avoidance
    - Strategies to Break Negative Cycles

3. Conflict Resolution for Real Relationships
    - Tailored Conflict Resolution Techniques
    - De-escalation Strategies for Heated Moments
    - Navigate Conflicts During Major Life Changes
    - Balance Emotions and Logic in Disputes
    - Steps to Rebuild and Repair After Conflict

4. The Power of Emotional Vulnerability
    - Build Trust Through Open Dialogue
    - Safe Spaces for Emotional Disclosure
    - Vulnerability Exercises for Couples
    - Rebuild Trust After Betrayal

5. Navigate Digital and Traditional Communication
    - Digital Communication as Friend or Foe
    - Strategies for a Healthy Digital Detox
    - Maintain Connection Across Distances
    - Digital Etiquette for Couples
    - Blend Digital and In-Person Communication

6. Customize Communication Styles for Compatibility
    - Discover Your Communication Style
    - Align Differing Communication Styles for Better Interaction
    - Overcome Misaligned Communication
    - Tailor Communication to Meet Individual Needs
    - Effective Techniques for Diverse Dynamics

7. Practical Exercises for Lasting Change
    - Active Listening Exercises for Daily Practice
    - Empathy-Building Activities for Couples
    - Conflict Resolution Role-Playing Scenarios
    - Mindful Communication Techniques
    - Expressing Appreciation

8. Build Resilience in Relationships
    - Resilience is the Foundation of Lasting Relationships
    - Adapt to Life's Changes Together
    - Emotional Flexibility Enables Bouncing Back from Setbacks

      Sustain Intimacy During Stressful Times
      Growth-Oriented Communication Practices

9. Embrace Inclusivity and Diverse Relationships
      Communication Strategies for Non-Traditional Relationships
      Inclusivity in Relationship Dynamics
      Address Cultural Differences in Communication
      Keep the Spark Alive in Long-Distance Love

10. Sustain Growth and Connection
      Set Relationship Goals Together
      Continuous Learning and Adaptation
      Build a Supportive Partnership Community
      Celebrate Milestones and Progress

Conclusion

References

Introduction

We've all been there. You and your partner start with a simple conversation about who forgot to take out the trash or what to watch on TV. But before you know it, you're in a heated argument. Voices are raised, feelings are hurt, and the original issue is long forgotten. It's a scenario many couples know all too well. It leaves you wondering: Why does this keep happening?

Welcome to "Couples Communication Code." This book is your guide to navigating these challenges, written with a deep understanding of your issues. We'll focus on helping you and your partner communicate more effectively so you can break free from these frustrating cycles.

Many of us struggle with emotional shutdowns or feel like we're walking on eggshells. Are you repeating the same argument repeatedly, wishing things could change? Is sharing your needs without being misunderstood possible? You're not alone; these questions are at the heart of what we're tackling here.

This book holds the promise of transformation. It's about moving toward conflict-free conversations and rediscovering the deep connection that brought you together. Yes, lasting love is within reach. It's about learning to talk without triggering each other and building trust that stands the test of time.

Let me introduce myself. My passion is helping couples overcome communication hurdles. I want to see you achieve more meaningful and lasting connections. These pages are dedicated to understanding these issues and providing practical, effective solutions.

This book will explore key themes like empathy, emotional intelligence, and effective conflict resolution. We'll also explore listening without reacting defensively and expressing needs with kindness. Each chapter will build on these themes, offering insights and exercises to help you grow.

The strategies in this book are backed by comprehensive research and authoritative insights. You're not getting just my thoughts; you're getting a wealth of knowledge from those who are skilled in couples' communication.

As you read, I encourage you to actively participate in your relationship. Reflect on your communication patterns and dynamics. What are the recurring themes? Where do you get stuck? This book is a journey of introspection and growth. It's about understanding yourself and your partner better.

Commitment is needed to this journey for success. Improving your communication and relationship quality takes effort, but the rewards are worth it. Engaging with the exercises and strategies in this book is a step toward a healthier, more connected relationship.

Your relationship doesn't have to be a battlefield. It can be a place of peace, connection, and love. Let's start this journey together. Let's move toward a brighter future where conversations are no longer a source of conflict but a pathway to understanding and intimacy.

Chapter One

Understand the Fundamentals of Communication

You might think you know your partner like the back of your hand until a simple disagreement spirals into a full-blown argument. Suddenly, you're speaking different languages, and nothing makes sense. You wonder if you're living with an alien rather than someone you love. It's like trying to tune into a radio station just out of range. The static gets louder, and you're not hearing each other. This chapter will untangle communication wires, helping you tune into each other with clarity and empathy.

Welcome to the heart of communication, where we unravel why we say what we say and how it lands with our partners. Understanding these fundamentals isn't just about talking more; it's about connecting on a deeper level, ensuring that messages are heard and truly understood. It's about transforming how you communicate, moving from confusion to clarity.

The Art of Empathy in Conversations

Empathy is the ability to step into someone else's shoes and see the world through their eyes. It's the cornerstone of effective communication between partners. But let's be clear—empathy isn't sympathy. Sympathy involves feeling sorry for someone. Empathy is about understanding and sharing their feelings. It's about forming a genuine emotional connection, which can transform conversations from surface-level exchanges to meaningful dialogues.

Empathy is not just a tool for understanding. It's a transformative force in relationships. When you practice empathy, you're not just hearing words; you're understanding the emotions behind them. This connection fosters trust and intimacy, allowing you to navigate conflicts with compassion rather than frustration. Empathy helps bridge the gap between you and your partner's worlds, facilitating a stronger, more connected relationship.

So, how do we build empathy in our daily lives? Start with empathy mapping, a technique that helps you visualize your partner's perspective. Imagine what they're feeling and thinking during a conversation. This practice shifts focus from your own reactions to understanding theirs. Mirroring emotions also plays a vital role. When your partner shares something, reflect their feelings back to them. If they say they're stressed, acknowledge it by saying, "I can see this is overwhelming for you." This validates their emotions and shows you're genuinely engaged.

Role-playing exercises can further enhance empathy. By switching roles and reenacting scenarios, you gain insight into how your partner perceives situations. It's not just about acting; it's about experiencing their viewpoint firsthand. This practice can dissolve misunderstandings and foster a deeper bond.

However, empathy doesn't always come easily. Emotional biases can cloud judgment, making it hard to empathize effectively. We view situations through our personal lens, which can create barriers. Recognizing these biases is crucial for overcoming them. Stress is another empathy killer. When you're overwhelmed, focusing on anything beyond your survival mode is tough. Taking time to manage stress ensures that you're present and open to understanding your partner's needs. It's also important to be aware of potential pitfalls of empathy, such as emotional burnout or over-identification, and take steps to avoid these.

When empathy thrives in a relationship, it transforms dynamics profoundly. Trust is built through empathetic listening, as partners feel heard and valued. When you acknowledge each other's emotions without judgment, you create a safe space where vulnerability is accepted and welcomed. This strengthens the foundation of your bond.

Empathy also plays a pivotal role in conflict resolution. Approaching disagreements empathetically allows for compassionate problem-solving rather than combative exchanges. You move from a space of defensiveness to understanding, paving the way for constructive dialogue.

Empathy Check-In

Take a moment to reflect on a recent conversation with your partner. Ask yourself these questions:

- "Did I truly understand their perspective?"
- "How did I respond to their emotions?"
- "What could I do differently next time?"
- Write down your thoughts in a journal.

This practice encourages self-awareness and growth in your empathetic abilities.

Empathy is more than just a skill; it's a way of being present with your partner in every interaction. By cultivating empathy intentionally, you lay the groundwork for deeper connections and healthier communication patterns that will enrich your relationship for years.

Understanding the fundamentals of communication begins with embracing empathy as an integral part of how you relate to each other. It's not always easy, but it's always worth it.

Build Emotional Intelligence Together

Emotional intelligence, or EI, is the secret sauce that makes relationships thrive. It's not just about being smart with your emotions; it's about understanding, managing, and using them to enhance your interactions with your partner. Think of EI as having three main ingredients: self-awareness, self-regulation, and motivation for personal growth. Self-awareness is about recognizing your emotions as they happen. It's the ability to say, "Hey, I'm feeling anxious right now," and understand why. Self-regulation follows, allowing you to manage those feelings effectively. Instead of letting anger dictate your actions, you pause, breathe, and respond calmly. Lastly, motivation drives you to grow and improve, not just for yourself but for the relationship as a whole.

When you and your partner work on building emotional intelligence together, you're setting the stage for more meaningful communication. One way to start is by journaling emotions. Spend a few minutes each day writing down what you felt and why. This practice helps you understand your emotional triggers and patterns. You can also explore emotional intelligence workshops or exercises. These structured activities provide a space to practice EI skills in a supportive environment. For instance, you can try the 'emotional check-in' exercise, where you both share your current emotional state and discuss how it might impact your interactions. They can be eye-opening experiences that reveal how you react under pressure and how to improve those reactions.

High emotional intelligence brings a host of benefits to relationships. It's not just about understanding and managing your own emotions but also about how you interact with your partner. For starters, it enhances conflict resolution. When both partners understand and manage their emotions well, disagreements don't escalate as quickly. Instead, they become opportunities for growth and understanding. Emotional resilience is another perk. Couples with high EI bounce back from setbacks faster, maintaining a strong connection even in tough times. And let's not forget the strengthened emotional bonds. Understanding and regulating your emotions creates a safe space for vulnerability and intimacy, deepening your connection.

But boosting EI isn't without its challenges. Emotional baggage from past experiences can weigh heavy, making it hard to develop these skills. It's crucial to acknowledge this baggage and address it head-on. Whether through therapy or open conversations with your partner, unpacking these issues is vital for progress. Another obstacle is resistance to change. Many people are set in their ways and feel uncomfortable stepping out of their emotional comfort zones. Overcoming this resistance requires patience and commitment to the process.

To tackle these challenges effectively, start by fostering an environment of openness and acceptance in your relationship. Encourage each other to express emotions freely without fear of judgment or criticism. This openness paves the way for honest discussions about past hurts and fears that could block emotional growth. It's essential to approach these conversations with empathy and understanding, recognizing that change takes time and effort.

Consider incorporating mindfulness practices into your daily routine as well. Mindfulness enhances self-awareness by keeping you present in the moment and attuned to your emotions as they arise. It helps you notice emotional patterns before they spiral out of control, allowing you to address them constructively. Simple mindfulness exercises, like deep breathing or meditation, can significantly affect your emotional regulation abilities.

Another strategy is to set clear goals for improving emotional intelligence as a couple. Discuss what aspects of emotional intelligence you want to enhance and create a plan to work on them together. These goals may include practicing active listening during conversations or regularly checking in with each other about emotional well-being. Having concrete objectives keeps you both accountable and focused on continuous improvement.

Remember to celebrate small victories as you develop your emotional intelligence as a team. Recognize when you've successfully navigated a difficult conversation or shown more patience and understanding toward each other. These moments of progress are essential milestones on your path to a more emotionally intelligent relationship.

Building emotional intelligence together is an ongoing process that requires dedication and effort from both partners. It's about learning to understand each other more meaningfully and cultivating an environment where both feel safe expressing their true selves. Through journaling, workshops, mindfulness, and open communication, you can overcome obstacles and enjoy the profound benefits that high EI brings to your relationship.

Active Listening Goes Beyond Just Hearing

Active listening is more than just letting sound waves hit your eardrums. It's a focused and mindful process, crucial for effective communication. Imagine watching a movie, but you only catch every other scene. You might get the gist but miss the nuances and depth. That's what hearing without listening does to your conversations. Hearing is passive, a physiological process of perceiving sound. Listening, especially active listening, involves engaging with the speaker, understanding their message, and responding thoughtfully. It requires you to be present in the moment, setting aside distractions and prejudices, to truly comprehend and connect with your partner.

Active listening plays a pivotal role in understanding. By truly listening, you move beyond surface-level exchanges into a deeper level of comprehending your partner's needs and emotions. It's the difference between knowing the words they're saying and grasping the feelings behind those words. Effective listening validates your partner's experience, fostering an environment where both feel understood and respected. The result is a more profound connection, where conversations build bridges instead of walls.

To practice active listening, start with reflective listening techniques. This involves paraphrasing or summarizing what your partner says to confirm understanding. For instance, if they express frustration about something, you might respond, "It sounds like you've been through a lot." This shows you're not just hearing but processing their words. Pay attention to non-verbal cues—body language, tone of voice, and facial expressions. They provide context that enriches the spoken message. Asking clarifying questions is another vital technique. These questions help you dig deeper into what your partner is saying, ensuring clarity. Questions like "Can you explain what you mean by that?" or "How did that make you feel?" signal your genuine interest in their perspective.

However, several barriers can impede active listening. Distractions and multitasking are major culprits. In today's fast-paced world, letting your mind wander or checking your phone while your partner speaks is easy. This split attention dilutes the quality of your listening. To overcome this, create a distraction-free zone during conversations—put away devices and focus entirely on the speaker.

Preconceived notions and judgments also obstruct listening. Suppose you've already made up your mind about what your partner is saying or why they're saying it. In that case, you're likely to misinterpret their message. It's essential to approach each conversation with an open mind, resisting the urge to jump to conclusions. Remember that active listening is about understanding, not judging.

Active listening has a profound impact on relationships. It builds trust as partners feel heard and valued. When you listen attentively, you affirm that their thoughts and feelings matter to you. This assurance strengthens the foundation of trust within the relationship. Furthermore, it enhances mutual respect and validation. By acknowledging and responding thoughtfully to your partner's expressions, you demonstrate respect for their experiences and emotions.

Active listening also transforms how conflicts are handled. Instead of reacting defensively or dismissively during disagreements, you engage in a dialogue where both parties feel understood. This shift reduces tensions and facilitates more constructive resolutions. Moreover, as trust and respect grow through active listening, intimacy deepens. Partners feel more comfortable sharing vulnerabilities when they know they won't be ignored or misunderstood.

Active listening isn't just a skill; it's a commitment to being fully present with your partner. It's choosing to value their words and emotions as much as yours. By embracing this practice, you open the door to richer communication and more profound connections in your relationship.

Identify and Bridge Empathy Gaps

Empathy gaps can be likened to invisible walls that form between partners, leading to emotional disconnects and misunderstandings. These gaps occur when one partner fails to understand or feel what the other is experiencing. It's like trying to watch a movie in another language without subtitles—you're missing the context, and the plot gets lost. Emotional disconnection arises when partners don't truly grasp each other's feelings, creating a chasm in communication. Misinterpretations follow, where intentions get twisted, and words lose their intended meaning, leaving both parties frustrated and unheard.

Bridging these empathy gaps requires intentional effort and strategies to close emotional divides. Regular emotional check-ins can act as a lifeline, allowing partners to sync up emotionally. Consider it a scheduled time when you ask each other, "How are we doing?" This practice opens up space for honest dialogue about feelings and concerns that might otherwise go unspoken. Engaging in joint activities also fosters connection. Whether cooking a meal together, taking a walk, or trying out a new hobby, these shared experiences cultivate a sense of unity and understanding. Encouraging open-ended discussions is key, too. Instead of questions that prompt yes or no answers, ask your partner about their thoughts or feelings on a topic. These discussions invite depth and insight, helping you understand each other more profoundly.

Empathy gaps often stem from various sources. Cultural differences can be significant, as diverse backgrounds bring different communication styles and expectations. It's essential to recognize and respect these differences while finding common ground. Emotional unavailability is another culprit. When one partner struggles to express emotions or is detached, it becomes challenging for the other to empathize. Addressing this involves fostering an environment where vulnerability is safe and welcomed. Encouraging your partner to share their emotions without fear of judgment can slowly dismantle these barriers.

Closing empathy gaps brings many benefits that enhance relationship satisfaction and emotional intimacy. When partners align emotionally, they experience increased emotional alignment, where both feel understood and valued. This alignment strengthens the emotional fabric of the relationship, fostering a sense of partnership and solidarity. Greater relationship satisfaction follows naturally as communication improves and misunderstandings diminish. When empathy flows freely, partners feel more connected, leading to a deeper bond that withstands challenges.

However, bridging empathy gaps isn't always straightforward. It requires patience, practice, and a willingness to step outside your comfort zone. Cultural differences can be addressed through education and open conversations about each other's backgrounds and experiences. Sharing stories from your upbringing or traditions can offer insight into how these influences shape your perspectives and behaviors today.

When dealing with emotional unavailability, it's crucial to approach the situation with compassion rather than criticism. Encourage your partner to explore their emotions at their own pace, offering support and understanding. You might want to suggest activities that promote self-reflection or seek guidance from a therapist if needed.

Another effective strategy is to create shared rituals that reinforce connection. These rituals can be as simple as a weekly date night where you dedicate time to each other without distractions. Over time, these consistent practices build trust and intimacy, naturally closing empathy gaps.

Mindfulness practices can also enhance empathy by keeping you present and attuned to your partner's needs. Mindful breathing exercises or meditation sessions can help cultivate awareness and emotional sensitivity.

Increased emotional alignment paves the way for greater relationship satisfaction by fostering an environment where both partners feel seen and appreciated. As empathy gaps close, conflicts decrease in frequency and intensity because both parties are more attuned to each other's needs.

Ultimately, bridging empathy gaps is about creating an atmosphere of openness, understanding, and acceptance within your relationship. It involves recognizing the invisible walls that separate you from your partner and taking deliberate steps to dismantle them piece by piece.

The Science of Emotional Connection

At the core of every thriving relationship lies the emotional bond that glues partners together, an intricate dance of psychological and biological processes. Attachment theory, rooted in early developmental psychology, reveals how our first relationships shape our adult connections. When you feel secure in a relationship, it's often because those early bonds laid a solid foundation. This theory explains why some partners cling to adulthood while others withdraw during conflicts. The invisible thread guides how we connect, love, and sometimes push each other away. Our brains also play a crucial role. Neurobiological responses to emotional stimuli dictate how we react to our partner's touch, words, or even their presence. These responses can trigger warmth and closeness or stress and anxiety, influencing how we perceive and connect with our partners daily.

Emotional connection isn't just a nice-to-have; it's vital for relationship health. When couples neglect this bond, they risk drifting apart, leading to emotional neglect that can be as damaging as more overt conflicts. It's like a garden left untended; weeds of resentment and misunderstanding begin to sprout. Conversely, when couples nurture their emotional connection, they create a reservoir of goodwill that buffers against life's inevitable stresses. Shared experiences are particularly potent in strengthening these bonds. Whether traveling together, tackling a home project, or simply watching a favorite show, these moments weave a rich tapestry of memories that reinforce the sense of being in it together.

So, how do you enhance this emotional connection? Begin with shared rituals and traditions. These can be as simple as a weekly date night or a morning coffee ritual. They act as anchors amidst life's chaos, reminding you of what truly matters. Consistently expressing gratitude is another powerful tool. A simple "thank you" for everyday gestures can transform the mundane into meaningful acts of love. Gratitude shifts focus from what's missing to what's present, fostering appreciation and warmth. Incorporating mindfulness practices can also deepen your connection. Mindfulness encourages presence, allowing you to savor each moment together without distraction. Whether through meditation or mindful breathing exercises, these practices help center your relationship amid life's demands.

Yet, maintaining emotional bonds isn't without its hurdles. Emotional distance can creep in over time, often unnoticed, until it feels like a chasm between you and your partner. Addressing past emotional wounds is also crucial. Unresolved pain can become a barrier to intimacy, preventing the vulnerability needed for proper connection. To manage emotional distance, prioritize regular check-ins with your partner. Ask open-ended questions about their feelings and experiences, creating space for honest dialogue. Recognize and validate each other's emotions without judgment, fostering an environment where both feel seen and heard.

Addressing past wounds requires courage and patience. It might involve difficult conversations or seeking professional help to navigate complex emotions. The key is approaching these discussions with empathy and a willingness to heal together. This openness paves the way for renewed intimacy and trust.

The obstacles to emotional connection are not insurmountable, but they require intentional effort and commitment from both partners. By recognizing these challenges and adopting strategies to overcome them, couples can cultivate a resilient emotional bond that endures through life's ups and downs.

Fostering emotional connection creates a relationship that not only survives but thrives. It's about building a home within each other where both feel safe, cherished and understood. This connection becomes the foundation upon which love grows stronger, enriching your lives beyond measure.

As you nurture this bond, remember that it's not about grand gestures but the small moments that count—the shared laughter, the comforting silence, and the knowing glance across a crowded room. These threads weave your lives together into a tapestry of love and understanding—a testament to the power of emotional connection in your relationship.

Chapter Two

Recognize and Break Negative Communication Patterns

Recognize High-Frequency Patterns of Frustration

Do you ever find yourself arguing about the same silly things repeatedly? Why is the laundry always left on the floor, or who forgot to pick up groceries? These aren't just random squabbles; they're high-frequency patterns of frustration. For instance, it could be about the way the dishes are washed or the frequency of cleaning the house. They're like an annoying song stuck on repeat, playing the same tune day in and day out. So, what exactly are these patterns, and why do they happen?

High-frequency frustration patterns are those recurring tiffs that seem insignificant but can blow up into something bigger. You might start with a minor issue, like dishes piling up, but it quickly spirals into a full-blown argument. Passive-aggressive behaviors often sneak into the mix, adding fuel to the fire. You could treat your partner silently or make sarcastic comments instead of addressing the problem head-on. Not surprisingly, these patterns tend to escalate rather than resolve the underlying tensions.

So, how do you spot these cycles before they cause more damage? Look for increased irritability. Are you quicker to snap at your partner over minor issues? Emotional withdrawal is another red flag. If you find yourself pulling away emotionally, it's a sign you're caught in a cycle. This withdrawal can create a chasm between you and your partner, leading to a lack of communication and intimacy.

The impact of these frustration patterns can be disastrous. Over time, they erode trust and intimacy, like water slowly wearing away a rock. You start feeling emotionally distant from each other as if you're living parallel lives rather than sharing one. Minor disagreements escalate quickly, turning your home into a battleground rather than a sanctuary.

It's crucial to identify your personal patterns to break free from these negative cycles. Start by journaling your daily interactions with your partner. What triggers these arguments? How do you react? Writing it down helps you see the bigger picture and identify recurring themes. Self-reflection exercises can also be enlightening. Set aside time each week to reflect on your communication style and consider what changes you can make.

Mapping Your Frustration Patterns

Grab a notebook and jot down recent arguments you've had. What were they about? How did you feel during those moments? Note any patterns or triggers you notice. This exercise encourages awareness and helps pinpoint areas for improvement.

By understanding these patterns of frustration, you're taking the first step toward healthier communication. It's about recognizing those pesky cycles and saying enough is enough. You're not alone in this struggle; many couples face similar challenges. But with awareness comes the power to change and grow together. This understanding brings a sense of relief, knowing that there's a way out of these frustrating cycles, and it can be a powerful motivator for change.

Breaking negative communication patterns requires effort and commitment from both partners. It's about engaging in honest conversations rather than falling back into old habits. By identifying high-frequency frustration patterns and their signs, you can address them before they damage your relationship. This shared responsibility creates a sense of unity, knowing you're working towards healthier communication.

Remember, you're not just battling your partner but teaming up against the problem. It's about working together to create a space where communication flows freely without fear of judgment or retaliation.

Taking responsibility for your actions and reactions is key to breaking these cycles. It's about acknowledging when you've slipped into passive-aggressive behaviors or allowed irritability to cloud your judgment. By holding each other accountable in a loving way, you foster an environment where growth and understanding thrive.

Know that change won't happen overnight. There will be setbacks, but every step forward brings you closer to healthier communication and a stronger bond. This reassurance can help you stay encouraged and resilient, knowing that change is possible and setbacks are just part of the journey.

Recognizing high-frequency frustration patterns is just one piece of the puzzle in breaking negative communication cycles. It's about learning from past experiences and using them as stepping stones toward building a more harmonious relationship.

The journey may be challenging at times, but remember that you're in it together—working hand in hand toward a brighter future filled with love, trust, and understanding.

Understand Your Partner's Emotional Triggers

Emotional triggers are like invisible buttons that, when pressed, can set off a chain reaction of intense feelings. These aren't just random emotional outbursts; they're deeply tied to past experiences and unresolved traumas. For example, suppose someone felt abandoned as a child. In that case, a partner's late arrival might trigger that old fear, sparking an outsized emotional response. Understanding these triggers is crucial for preventing conflict because they often operate in the shadows, catching both partners off guard.

Identifying emotional triggers requires keen observation and honest communication. Pay attention to patterns in your emotional responses. Is there a recurring situation where you or your partner consistently react with anger, sadness, or anxiety? These reactions often hint at underlying triggers. Openly discussing past experiences can also shed light on these hidden influences. Sharing stories from your past, especially those that were painful or significant, allows your partner to understand why certain things might set you off. It's about creating a safe space where both of you feel comfortable exploring your emotional histories without fear of judgment or ridicule.

Empathy plays a pivotal role in managing these triggers once they're identified. It's about stepping into your partner's shoes and seeing the world through their eyes. During sensitive discussions, practice active listening. This means not just hearing words but truly understanding the feelings behind them. When your partner talks about their triggers, validate their feelings by acknowledging their experiences. Phrases like "I can see why that would upset you" or "I understand why this is hard for you" show you care and are willing to support them. This validation doesn't just soothe immediate tensions; it builds trust over time.

Addressing emotional triggers involves strategic planning and calming techniques. Develop a 'trigger plan' together for conflict prevention. This plan is like a roadmap for what to do when a trigger is activated. It could include agreeing to take a break if things get heated, using specific words to signal understanding, or having a go-to calming phrase to recenter yourselves. Calming techniques like deep breathing, meditation, or physical exercise can also help manage the physiological response often accompanying emotional triggers. Taking a few deep breaths can lower stress levels and bring clarity when emotions run high. This approach helps prevent knee-jerk reactions and allows for more thoughtful responses.

Trigger Mapping

Think back on recent situations where you felt emotionally triggered. What were the circumstances? How did you react? Write down any patterns or common themes you notice. This exercise encourages self-awareness and helps both partners better understand each other's vulnerabilities.

Understanding and managing emotional triggers is about building a partnership where both feel seen and heard. It's not just about avoiding arguments but about creating a relationship where empathy and understanding are at the forefront. By recognizing these triggers and working together to address them, you're laying the foundation for a more harmonious connection.

Remember that identifying and addressing emotional triggers is ongoing. It requires patience, openness, and a willingness to learn from each other. Over time, as you become more attuned to each other's needs and sensitivities, conflicts will diminish, replaced by deeper understanding and intimacy.

This journey involves both partners taking responsibility for their emotional health and supporting each other in moments of vulnerability. It's about moving beyond surface-level interactions and engaging in meaningful dialogue that fosters growth and connection.

By embracing empathy and developing strategies to manage emotional triggers, you create an environment where both partners feel valued and supported. This strengthens your bond and paves the way for healthier communication patterns that will benefit your relationship in the long run.

How to Break the Blame Loop

The blame loop is an everyday communication trap many couples fall into, often without realizing it. It begins with assigning fault instead of seeking solutions and quickly spirals into a cycle of defensiveness. Imagine it as a tennis match where you're both volleying accusations back and forth instead of playing together. Each time you blame your partner, you serve another shot, and this back-and-forth keeps the game going without ever resolving anything. This cycle only worsens conflicts, making reaching mutual understanding or resolution difficult.

Recognizing when you're in a blame loop is the first step to getting out of it. Frequent accusations are a clear sign; if every conversation seems to end with "it's your fault," you're likely stuck in this loop. Another indicator is defensiveness in response to feedback. When either partner instinctively defends themselves rather than listens, tension increases, preventing productive dialogue. These patterns create an environment where neither feels heard nor valued, leading to more misunderstandings.

Moving past blame requires a shift in mindset and communication style. Instead of saying, "You always do this," try using "I" statements, such as "I feel upset when this happens." This approach focuses on expressing personal feelings rather than assigning blame. Doing so invites your partner to understand your perspective without feeling attacked. Additionally, focus on problem-solving rather than fault-finding. Ask questions like, "How can we address this issue together?" This encourages collaboration and reduces the adversarial nature of discussions.

Breaking the blame loop offers numerous benefits for your relationship. Increased cooperation becomes possible when both partners focus on solutions instead of pointing fingers. This cooperative approach fosters a sense of teamwork, making it easier to tackle challenges together. Moreover, improved emotional safety is a significant outcome. When blame is removed from the equation, neither partner feels under attack, allowing for more open and honest communication. This environment of trust and safety is essential for nurturing intimacy and connection.

One practical strategy to help shift away from blame involves setting aside time for regular check-ins with each other. During these conversations, focus on discussing feelings and experiences without judgment. Use this time to share what's been on your mind and how certain situations have affected you emotionally. Encourage your partner to do the same, creating a space where both feel comfortable expressing themselves openly.

Another practical approach is developing a list of shared goals prioritizing communication improvement. Sit down together and identify areas where you'd like to see change or growth in your relationship. For example, you may want to work on active listening or practice empathy more consistently. These goals provide direction and motivation for breaking the blame loop and fostering healthier communication patterns.

Accountability also plays a crucial role in transforming how you communicate with each other. Hold yourself responsible for your actions and reactions during disagreements. Acknowledge when you've slipped into blaming behaviors and commit to making adjustments moving forward. Encourage your partner to do the same by establishing mutual accountability agreements outlining respectful communication expectations.

As you implement these strategies, remember that change takes time and patience from both partners. There will be moments when old habits resurface. Still, every effort toward breaking the blame loop brings you closer to a more harmonious relationship.

The path forward involves embracing a mindset of empathy and understanding rather than criticism and defensiveness. By focusing on expressing feelings constructively through "I" statements, seeking collaborative solutions, and fostering an environment of emotional safety, you pave the way for healthier interactions with each other.

Ultimately, breaking the blame loop creates space for deeper connection and lasting love. In this environment, both partners feel valued, understood, and committed to growing together as a team.

Overcome Communication Avoidance

Communication avoidance is like sweeping dust under the rug. It might seem clean on the surface, but eventually, you trip over the pile. This avoidance happens when you dodge those tough conversations or suppress feelings because they're uncomfortable. You know those talks where you're afraid of what might come out if you start. It could be about finances, family, or unmet needs. By not addressing these issues, you undermine the growth of your relationship. It's like building a house on a shaky foundation; eventually, it all crumbles.

Why do we shy away from these conversations? Fear of conflict tops the list. Nobody likes the idea of a shouting match or the silent treatment that might follow. Then there's the lack of confidence in expressing needs. You might worry about coming off as needy or demanding. It's easier to stay silent and hope things improve independently, but they rarely magically resolve without intervention. Avoidance might feel safe, but it's a ticking time bomb waiting to explode at the slightest provocation.

So, how do you tackle what you've been avoiding? Start by setting up a safe environment for dialogue. Find a quiet space where neither of you feels threatened or rushed. Turn off distractions like phones and TV. This setting tells your partner that this time is essential and dedicated to them. When you're ready to talk, use conversation starters to ease into topics. Say something like, "I've been thinking about..." or "Can we chat about..." These openers create a gentle entry point into difficult discussions.

When you finally confront what you've been avoiding, you open the door to healthier communication and stronger bonds. Greater transparency is one of the first benefits you'll notice. There's less room for assumptions and misunderstandings when everything's out in the open. This transparency naturally leads to enhanced trust as you feel more comfortable sharing your thoughts and feelings. Mutual understanding blossoms when you're willing to face challenges together rather than ignoring them.

As an example, let's say you've been worried about finances but haven't said anything because it feels awkward. The bills are piling up, and stress is mounting. Instead of holding it in, you sit down with your partner and discuss it openly. The conversation might start awkwardly, but there's relief once you both express your worries and brainstorm solutions. You feel like a team rather than adversaries hiding behind walls of silence.

The benefits of addressing communication avoidance extend beyond just resolving issues. You create a culture of openness in your relationship, where both feel valued and heard. This openness fosters an environment where both are encouraged to raise concerns before they fester into more significant problems. It's like regularly tidying your home instead of waiting until it's overwhelming—you maintain order and peace.

By embracing vulnerability and discussing complex topics, you strengthen your emotional connection. It's not just about solving problems; it's about building intimacy through shared experiences and mutual support. This process requires patience and courage from both partners, but every step toward facing avoidance brings you closer together.

Keep in mind that overcoming communication avoidance is an ongoing effort. It involves regularly checking in with each other about feelings and concerns rather than waiting for issues to escalate. Ask questions like "Is there anything on your mind that we should discuss?" or "How are we doing?" These check-ins create opportunities for dialogue and prevent problems from slipping through the cracks.

This journey requires both partners to be committed to growth and understanding. There will be times when old habits resurface. Still, every effort toward overcoming avoidance brings you closer to a healthier relationship.

Know that addressing communication avoidance is about choosing connection over fear. It's about opening up pathways for honest conversations that deepen your bond and enrich your relationship beyond measure.

Strategies to Break Negative Cycles

Negative communication cycles are like a stubborn knot in a shoelace. They involve recurrent themes in arguments and consistent emotional responses that keep the tension alive. Picture a couple arguing about the same issue repeatedly, never finding a resolution. It feels like a broken record, where grievances are aired without change in sight. These cycles thrive on predictability and feed off unresolved emotions, keeping both partners trapped in a conflict loop. Identifying these characteristics is the first step toward breaking free. Once you recognize them, you can see where things go wrong and why they keep repeating.

To disrupt these cycles, try implementing regular relationship check-ins. Think of them as mini-meetings with your partner to discuss what's working and what's not. These check-ins create a safe space for honest dialogue, allowing you to voice concerns before they become significant issues. Setting shared goals for communication improvement is also crucial. Whether committing to listen more actively or reducing the frequency of arguments, having common objectives gives you a direction to work toward. This proactive approach interrupts the negative patterns and replaces them with constructive habits.

Accountability plays a significant role in changing communication patterns. It involves taking responsibility for your actions and reactions. Personal accountability exercises can help you reflect on your behavior and its impact on the relationship. Consider keeping a journal where you note instances where you might have contributed to a conflict. This reflection fosters self-awareness and encourages growth. Partner accountability agreements take this a step further, where both of you agree to hold each other accountable in a supportive manner. These agreements promote mutual respect and ensure both parties commit to positive change.

Breaking negative cycles rejuvenates the relationship in ways that go beyond just reducing conflicts. You'll notice a renewed connection as both partners feel heard and valued. When you tackle issues together, it strengthens your bond and enhances cooperation. With improved communication, you start operating as a team, working through challenges rather than against each other. This partnership fosters an environment where love and understanding flourish, making the relationship more resilient to external pressures.

As you dismantle these negative patterns, your relationship will transform into a source of joy rather than stress. The effort you put into breaking these cycles pays off as you experience greater harmony and satisfaction. This transformation isn't just about resolving conflicts; it's about creating a relationship that supports both partners' growth and happiness.

In conclusion, breaking negative communication cycles requires both partners' awareness, strategy, and commitment. It's about identifying the patterns that hold you back and replacing them with healthier alternatives. As you move forward, remember that every small step contributes to creating a loving and supportive relationship.

Reflect on the changes you've started to implement and your progress. Recognizing and breaking negative cycles is an ongoing process that requires patience and dedication. In the next chapter, we'll explore how to deepen your emotional connection with your partner, building on the foundation you've created here. We'll continue strengthening your relationship, paving the way for lasting love and understanding.

Chapter Three

Conflict Resolution for Real Relationships

Tailored Conflict Resolution Techniques

You're in the kitchen, and a simple comment about the dishes spirals into a full-blown argument. The same old complaints surface and both of you retreat to your corners, wondering how you got here again. You're stuck in a loop, and breaking free feels impossible. But there's hope. Understanding different conflict resolution styles can be a game-changer, turning heated debates into productive discussions and bringing a sense of relief that there's a way out of this cycle.

Let's explore some common styles. Collaborative problem-solving is all about working together to find a solution that benefits both parties. It's like teaming up to solve a puzzle, where each piece represents a concern or need. This style thrives in relationships built on mutual respect and open dialogue. On the other hand, compromising is like meeting in the middle. It's about finding a quick resolution where both sides give a little, like agreeing on a movie when you can't decide between two. Each style has its place, and knowing when to use them is key.

Identifying your preferred conflict resolution style can be enlightening and empowering. You might naturally lean toward one method without even realizing it. Taking a conflict resolution style assessment can provide insight into your tendencies, giving you a sense of control over your reactions. These assessments help you understand whether you're more collaborative or prefer quick compromises. They can also highlight areas for growth, guiding you toward more effective ways of handling disputes. Recognizing your style is the first step in tailoring your approach to fit your relationship dynamics.

Flexibility in conflict resolution is crucial. Imagine always using the same approach, regardless of the situation—it's like trying to fix everything with a hammer when sometimes you need a wrench. Balancing assertiveness with cooperativeness allows you to adapt based on what's happening. Sometimes, standing firm is necessary, but other times, bending a little makes all the difference. It's essential to recognize when to change tactics for the best results.

Now, let's get practical with some actionable techniques for each style. For collaborative problem-solving, consider brainstorming sessions as a team. Sit down together and list potential solutions without judgment. It's about creating a safe space where ideas flow freely, leading to innovative solutions that satisfy both partners' needs. In contrast, creating win-win scenarios through negotiation involves finding a middle ground quickly. It's not about winning or losing but ensuring both parties leave the conversation feeling heard and valued.

Conflict Resolution Style Assessment

Conduct a brief assessment together to better understand your conflict resolution tendencies. Reflect on past disputes: How did you approach them? Were you more inclined to collaborate or compromise? Discuss your findings with your partner to align your strategies moving forward, fostering a sense of unity and shared understanding.

Remember, these techniques aren't one-size-fits-all. Sometimes, you must combine elements from different styles to achieve the best outcome. The key is being open to change and experimenting with new approaches. Doing so creates an environment where conflicts become opportunities for growth rather than battlegrounds.

As you explore these techniques, remember that conflict resolution is an ongoing process requiring effort and commitment from both partners. It's about recognizing that disagreements are part of any relationship but don't have to be destructive. With the right tools and mindset, you can transform how you handle conflicts, paving the way for stronger connections and lasting love.

Navigating conflicts requires patience, understanding, and adaptability. By embracing these tailored techniques, you're not just resolving disputes—you're building a foundation for healthier communication and deeper intimacy with your partner.

De-escalation Strategies for Heated Moments

You can feel your heart racing, your palms sweaty, and words spilling out before you can catch them. It's easy for a disagreement to quickly become a full-blown argument. This is why de-escalation matters so much. By reducing emotional intensity, you maintain a safe space for communication. It's about keeping the conversation from becoming a shouting match where no one feels heard. Think of de-escalation as a pressure valve, releasing steam before things boil over. When you calm the storm, you ensure that both feel comfortable continuing the dialogue without fear of it spiraling out of control.

Specific tactics can immediately cool things down in the heat of the moment. Taking a "time-out" is one such strategy. It's perfectly okay to step away and gather your thoughts. This isn't about avoiding the issue but ensuring you're constructively ready to engage when you return. Deep breathing exercises also work wonders. They slow your heart rate and shift focus away from anger, making it easier to engage calmly. Simple calming affirmations like "This too shall pass" can ground you, reminding you that the current tension is temporary and surmountable.

For more lasting peace, developing long-term de-escalation skills is vital. Establishing conflict boundaries with your partner sets clear expectations. It may mean agreeing not to raise voices or avoiding interrupting each other. These boundaries create a framework for respectful dialogue. Emotional regulation techniques also play a crucial role. This involves recognizing and managing your emotional state before it gets out of hand. It might mean practicing mindfulness or regular self-care to maintain emotional balance.

Self-awareness is another core element in de-escalation. Understanding what triggers your reactions allows better conflict management. Reflect on past disagreements: What set you off? What could have been handled differently? This reflection provides insights that inform future interactions. Monitoring emotional cues before they escalate offers early warning signs that you're getting worked up. Acknowledging these cues can prevent saying things in the heat of the moment you'll regret later.

Reflecting on past conflicts can be an enlightening exercise. Recall a recent argument and jot down what triggered your responses. Were there any signs you ignored? What emotions bubbled up? This reflection helps you pinpoint patterns and prepares you for future encounters.

These strategies help create a communication environment where both feel valued and heard. By integrating immediate tactics with long-term skills, you're not just putting out fires; you're preventing them from starting in the first place. This proactive approach ensures that discussions remain productive and that partners stay engaged without fear or resentment.

Remember, de-escalation isn't about avoiding issues but addressing them thoughtfully and respectfully. It requires effort, patience, and commitment from both partners to foster an environment where healthy communication thrives, even in difficult moments. Through these practices, conflicts become opportunities for growth and understanding rather than obstacles to overcome.

Incorporating these de-escalation strategies into your relationship toolkit can transform how you navigate disputes, creating a more harmonious connection with your partner. With practice and dedication, you'll discover that maintaining peace during heated moments strengthens your bond, paving the way for deeper intimacy and lasting love.

Navigate Conflicts During Major Life Changes

Life transitions are those times when everything seems to shift. One minute you're cruising along, and the next, you're dealing with new challenges. Take becoming parents, for instance. Suddenly, you're not just partners but co-parents, making decisions about bedtime routines and diaper brands. These changes can stir up parenting disagreements that weren't even on your radar before. Who knew you'd debate the merits of cloth versus disposable diapers at 2 a.m.? Then, there's the financial stress that comes with career changes. You might argue over budgets and expenses as you adjust to a new job or a reduced income. These common conflicts can feel overwhelming, but they don't have to be relationship-ending.

To manage these transitional conflicts, setting clear expectations and roles is crucial. Imagine starting a new job without knowing your responsibilities. Chaos, right? The same goes for relationships. Sit down with your partner and discuss who'll handle what. You may take on more household chores while the other focuses on work during this busy season. Regular check-ins are also vital. They keep you aligned on goals and provide space to voice concerns before they snowball into more significant issues. These check-ins are mini-tune-ups for your relationship, ensuring everything runs smoothly.

Flexibility becomes your best friend during life changes. Plans that once worked might no longer fit, requiring adjustments. Suppose your partner gets a promotion that demands more time at the office. You should juggle your schedule to manage the new dynamic at home. Keeping communication channels open is key here. Talk about what's working and what isn't, and be willing to adapt as needed. It's not always easy, but being open to change helps gracefully navigate these turbulent times.

Sometimes, outside support provides the perspective needed during transitions. Counseling or therapy offers a safe space to explore these new challenges with a professional who understands relationship dynamics. It's not about admitting defeat but strengthening your bond with expert guidance. Community groups also offer support, connecting you with others experiencing similar changes. Sharing stories and solutions with those who get it can be incredibly reassuring.

Picture a couple transitioning to parenthood for the first time, overwhelmed by sleepless nights and endless diaper changes. They've set clear roles—one handles night feedings while the other tackles morning duties—yet tension bubbles up over shared responsibilities. They schedule weekly check-ins to discuss their feelings and what adjustments might help. Through open dialogue, they realize flexibility is crucial, allowing them to swap roles when they feel burnt out.

Now imagine another couple facing financial strain after one partner loses their job. Arguments erupt over spending habits until they sit down and create a budget together, setting clear expectations for both parties. They agree on regular money talks to address concerns early rather than letting resentment build. With established open communication channels, they navigate this tough period without tearing them apart.

In both scenarios, adaptability plays a starring role in handling conflict during life changes. It's about recognizing that what once worked might need tweaking and being okay with that. Resources like therapy or community support further strengthen your ability to weather these storms together.

Navigating conflicts during significant life changes requires patience and understanding from both partners. It involves recognizing that these transitions are temporary but can have lasting impacts if not addressed thoughtfully. By setting clear expectations, maintaining open communication channels, and seeking support when needed, you create an environment where your relationship thrives despite the chaos surrounding you.

As you continue exploring how to navigate conflicts during notable life changes, remember that every couple faces challenges unique to their circumstances—and that's okay! Embrace these moments as opportunities for growth rather than obstacles standing in your way.

Balance Emotions and Logic in Disputes

Conflicts often feel like a tug-of-war between emotions and logic. On one side, emotions surge, clouding judgment and fueling intense reactions. Conversely, logic tries to steer the conversation towards reason and clarity. Both play a pivotal role in how conflicts unfold and resolve. Emotional responses can be immediate and raw, often stemming from deeply ingrained experiences or past wounds. They can drive the conversation in the wrong direction, making it hard to reach a resolution. In contrast, logical reasoning seeks structure and insight, offering a pathway to understanding and agreement. But too much logic can sometimes dismiss genuine feelings, leaving them unaddressed.

Balancing these forces requires acknowledging emotions first. Before diving into problem-solving mode, take a moment to recognize what you're feeling and why. It's like giving your feelings a name tag at a crowded event, helping you understand their place in the discussion. This acknowledgment doesn't mean letting emotions take the wheel entirely; instead, it ensures they have a seat at the table. Once feelings are validated, logic can guide the conversation toward resolution. Implementing "cooling-off" periods can also aid in regaining perspective. Taking a break allows both partners to step back, breathe, and return with a clearer mindset when tensions rise.

The interactions between emotions and logic lead to healthier conflict resolution. They pave the way for more equitable solutions where both parties feel heard and understood. When emotions are acknowledged, and logic is applied thoughtfully, decisions that respect both partners' perspectives emerge. This balance reduces emotional fallout, preventing lingering resentment or frustration from unresolved issues. It transforms disputes from battles into opportunities for growth and deeper connection.

Yet, achieving this balance isn't always easy. Emotional flooding can overwhelm, making it challenging to think straight or articulate needs clearly. It's like a tidal wave crashing over reason, leaving chaos in its wake. To combat this, practice emotional regulation techniques such as deep breathing or mindfulness exercises that help calm the storm within. Conversely, an over-reliance on rationality can lead to dismissing emotions as irrelevant or insignificant. This approach often leaves one partner feeling invalidated or unheard.

Overcoming these barriers involves developing emotional intelligence and recognizing when to switch gears from emotion to logic or vice versa. This adaptability is crucial for navigating conflicts with grace and understanding. Both partners must remain open to each other's experiences while respecting differing viewpoints.

During disputes, consider pausing to listen so each partner has the opportunity to express their thoughts and feelings without interruption. This practice fosters empathy by allowing both parties to see things from each other's perspective before transitioning into solution-focused discussions. It encourages active listening and cultivates a sense of partnership in addressing issues.

Another strategy involves setting aside dedicated times for discussing ongoing concerns outside of heated moments—perhaps weekly check-ins where you both can explore what's been on your mind without the pressure of immediate resolution. These conversations provide a safe space for expressing emotions freely while adding logical reasoning into potential solutions.

When you find yourself stuck in the throes of emotion or logic during a conflict, remember that achieving balance is an ongoing process that requires patience and practice from both partners. It's about fluidly learning to dance between these elements rather than letting one dominate the other entirely.

As you go through this chapter, know that balancing emotions and logic is not about erasing one in favor of the other but embracing both as valuable components of healthy conflict resolution. By including these elements thoughtfully into your interactions with your partner, you create an environment where understanding flourishes even amidst disagreement.

In doing so, you strengthen your ability to communicate openly and honestly with each other, transforming conflicts into opportunities for growth and connection rather than obstacles.

Steps to Rebuild and Repair After Conflict

When a conflict leaves emotional bruises, the path to healing can seem daunting. It is natural to feel a sense of trepidation when faced with mending what feels broken; however, much like tending to a garden after a fierce storm, repairing relationship damage necessitates an intentional, thoughtful approach. Offering sincere apologies serves as the foundational step. An apology transcends mere words like "I'm sorry"—it embodies a deeper acknowledgment of the hurt inflicted and an earnest acceptance of responsibility for one's actions. It is an extended olive branch, boldly signifying, "I highly value you and our relationship, and I am committed to making amends." However, words must be matched with actions; re-establishing trust relies on demonstrating consistent commitment over time. Trust, in its essence, is much like a fragile yet resilient plant—it thrives with regular nurturing through steadfast honesty and unwavering reliability. Show your partner that you are someone they can undoubtedly rely on by diligently keeping promises, offering support consistently, and being present in joyful moments and challenging times.

Forgiveness occupies an indispensable role in mending relationships. Contrary to popular belief, it does not entail erasing the past but rather making a conscious choice to release grudges that become burdens too heavy to bear. Embracing forgiveness as a transformative process helps one assimilate it fully. It begins with acknowledging the hurt, permitting oneself to experience the gamut of emotions, and then deciding to let them go. Self-forgiveness bears equal importance; clinging to guilt can hinder progress, so grant yourself the grace to err and evolve from those experiences. Likewise, practice partner forgiveness by shifting focus toward their admirable qualities and reaffirming the reasons you cherish your relationship.

Trust requires time and careful attention to rebuild, but practical exercises can expedite this journey. Engage with trust-building activities such as sharing personal insights or setting achievable goals together. These initiatives reinforce commendable behaviors and reiterate the mutual commitment between both partners. Consider engaging in activities necessitating cooperation, like preparing a meal together or starting a home project. These shared endeavors cultivate teamwork and foster mutual reliance, fortifying your relationship.

Creating a positive conflict history invites learning valuable lessons from past disputes to enhance future interactions. Maintaining a conflict resolution journal can offer profound insights. Chronicle what transpired, your emotional landscape, and the lessons gleaned from each conflict. This practice fosters reflection and growth but also aids in recognizing recurring patterns and tweaking them for improved outcomes. Celebrate the triumphs of successful resolutions, too, irrespective of their size. Acknowledging the progress achieved and the skills honed during these times is crucial.

Trust-Building

Engage in a simple yet profound trust-building exercise: Dedicate a designated time each week to sharing something new about yourselves with each other—be it a cherished story from your past or a dream for the future. This practice nurtures intimacy and deepens trust by fostering an environment of openness and vulnerability.

As this chapter draws to a close, it is vital to remind yourself that rebuilding after a conflict remains an incremental, albeit rewarding, process that calls on both partners to exhibit patience and unwavering dedication. It means taking small, purposeful steps toward healing and growth instead of seeking immediate change. With earnest apologies, embracing forgiveness wholeheartedly, and actively participating in trust-building exercises, you can cultivate an environment where love and resilience can thrive anew.

The journey of repairing relationship damage goes beyond mere mending what is broken; it involves forging a fortified foundation for enduring resilience in the face of adversities. Every step toward healing elevates you closer to nurturing a profound connection with your partner, constructed on trust, deep understanding, and mutual respect. As we advance to the next chapter, we will focus on deepening emotional intimacy in your relationship by establishing secure spaces for vulnerability and authentic connection. This exploration will build on a solid foundation, steering you toward a more gratifying partnership full of love and mutual comprehension.

Chapter Four

The Power of Emotional Vulnerability

Let's say you're sitting comfortably across from your partner in a space filled with warmth and familiarity. You're about to share a significant story from your formative years—a story that, despite its importance, you've kept hidden, like an old, cherished photograph tucked away in a forgotten drawer. As you delve into the narrative, recounting each detail, you notice your voice quivering slightly. It's a moment that reveals your raw, unfiltered self, a moment of vulnerability and profound liberation. This scenario encapsulates the very essence of emotional vulnerability. It's about presenting the entirety of your being—blemishes, quirks, and all—to the one you cherish the most. Embracing this vulnerability does more than strengthen your connection; it transforms it from a simple companionship into a deep, lasting alliance built on trust and shared understanding. When you open your heart, you invite your partner to explore the depths of your being, cultivating a bond that extends beyond words.

Yet, we must be honest—taking the plunge into vulnerability can be intimidating. The possibility of being rejected or misjudged often feels daunting, casting a shadow over the idea of opening up. No one wishes to expose their innermost self only to encounter indifference or criticism. It is easy to misinterpret vulnerability as synonymous with weakness, erroneously believing that showing genuine emotion is like admitting a lack of strength. However, vulnerability is anything but a weakness. It is a demonstration of bravery, indicating that you possess the fortitude to risk so much for sincerity and genuine connection. You are essentially communicating, "This is my true self—accept me as I am or not at all." This authentic proclamation is profoundly powerful and a testament to your courage.

When individuals embrace vulnerability, they unlock many benefits that transform relationships into more genuine and rewarding engagements. Lowering defenses allows emotional closeness to flourish organically. Your partner then feels warmly invited into the private sanctum of your world, which nurtures empathy and fosters understanding. Such openness gives rise to an ambiance where both partners experience being cherished and loved not for who they aspire to be but for who they truly are, imperfections included. As each layer of the façade gradually dissolves, partners fortify the cornerstone for enduring intimacy. The rewards of vulnerability are immense and worth the initial discomfort.

Steps to Practicing Vulnerability

To develop a practice of vulnerability, start by sharing personal narratives and adventures, illustrating your life experiences to each other. These stories can range as broadly as a treasured memory from your youth, a significant life event, or a recent challenge faced at your employment. The learning lies in relaying these events without fear of repercussions or judgment. It's all about conveying the truth, not creating a flawless account.

Articulating your emotions with sincerity is another pivotal element in forging deeper connections. For instance, should you feel anxious or distressed, express it authentically and allow those sensitive emotions to surface unimpeded by the rush to find solutions or fears of judgment. You can use 'I' statements to express your feelings, such as 'I feel anxious when...' or 'I'm distressed because...'. Such expression enhances the bond, rendering it more genuine and resilient.

Vulnerability Consideration

Take some time in stillness to contemplate a moment when you experienced vulnerability in the presence of your partner. What was it that you chose to share? Carefully consider how this openness shaped your relationship. Document your reflections in a journal in full detail. This exercise promotes self-awareness, encouraging you to pinpoint growth areas where vulnerability can flourish.

Regularly practicing these techniques lets you observe nuanced changes in your interactions and dialogues. Conversations gain depth, and exchanges feel more sincere. The former barriers of miscommunication gradually erode, giving way to mutual trust like petals blooming in the rays of understanding. Committing to regular open communication is a sign of your dedication to your relationship, and it's a step towards a healthier, more fulfilling connection.

While traversing the landscape of vulnerability may initially appear challenging, it's essential to acknowledge that this path is an evolving journey rather than a set goal. Each modest step toward transparency fortifies the emotional connection not just between you and your partner but also within yourself. By persistently practicing vulnerability as a lifestyle habit, you cultivate a fertile ground where authentic relationships grow lushly—a place where love thrives amidst honest interaction and compassionate awareness.

So embrace this opportunity—immerse yourself in emotional vulnerability with your partner beside you, and explore the transformative potential it offers for nurturing a profound connection that is, indeed, immeasurable.

Build Trust Through Open Dialogue

Imagine sitting with your partner and discussing your day, dreams, or fears. This openness is where trust begins. Transparent communication is like the mortar holding the bricks of your relationship together. You build a foundation that can withstand time and turmoil when you're consistently honest in conversations. Openly sharing thoughts and feelings isn't just about talking; it's about inviting your partner into your world, allowing them to understand you on a deeper level. This transparency fosters a sense of security and reliability, creating a space where both of you feel safe to express yourselves without fear of judgment or misunderstanding.

Open dialogue isn't always easy. Many obstacles can stand in the way. Fear of conflict or disagreement often silences us, making us avoid overly daunting conversations. Nobody likes the idea of turning a calm evening into an argument. Additionally, cultural or personal communication norms can act as barriers. Perhaps you grew up in an environment where keeping emotions to yourself was the norm or expressing feelings was seen as a sign of weakness. Overcoming these hurdles requires intentionality and commitment to change. Recognizing these barriers is the first step toward breaking them down and fostering an environment where open dialogue can thrive.

To encourage this openness, setting regular 'open talk' sessions can be incredibly beneficial. These are dedicated times when both partners can voice their thoughts and feelings without interruption or defensiveness. It's a practice that demands patience and active listening. Start by scheduling these sessions weekly or biweekly, ensuring they become a regular part of your relationship routine. During these sessions, each partner should have the opportunity to speak without interruption, and the other should listen actively and without judgment. Encourage feedback without jumping to defense mode. This might mean practicing restraint when you hear something you don't like or pausing before responding to ensure you're truly listening. These strategies build a habit of honesty and transparency in your day-to-day interactions.

The benefits of maintaining open lines of communication are immense. Trust grows stronger when each partner feels understood and valued. It's like watering a plant; regular nurturing helps it flourish. Open dialogue reduces misunderstandings and assumptions, preventing minor issues from snowballing into larger problems. When both partners are committed to honest communication, there's less room for doubt or suspicion. This clarity enhances the relationship's health, making it more resilient against external pressures and internal challenges.

Open dialogue strengthens trust and reliability, allowing both partners to lean on each other during challenging times. This mutual support creates a sense of partnership and teamwork, enhancing the overall quality of the relationship. Couples who prioritize open communication often find themselves more aligned in their goals and values, working together toward a common vision for their future.

Overcoming barriers to open dialogue requires effort and patience, but the rewards are worth it. As you practice these strategies, remember that building trust is an ongoing process that evolves over time. It's about creating an environment where both partners feel safe to express themselves honestly and openly without fear of judgment or rejection.

Incorporating open dialogue into your relationship may require some adjustment, especially if you're not used to regularly sharing your thoughts and feelings. Be patient with yourself and your partner as you navigate this new territory together. It's okay if things don't go perfectly at first; what matters is your commitment to growth and understanding.

As you prioritize open communication in your relationship, take note of the positive changes that occur over time. Trust deepens naturally as both partners become more attuned to each other's needs and desires. This deeper connection fosters a sense of intimacy that enriches every aspect of your relationship.

Building trust through open dialogue is ultimately about choosing authenticity over pretense and connection over distance. It requires vulnerability and courage from both partners but offers profound rewards in return. By embracing this practice wholeheartedly, you pave the way for a healthier, more fulfilling relationship that thrives on honesty, understanding, and mutual respect.

Safe Spaces for Emotional Disclosure

You're sitting with your partner; the air between you feels light and welcoming. This is a safe space—a non-judgmental and supportive environment where both of you can speak freely without the fear of criticism or dismissal. It's where mutual respect and understanding are the pillars holding up every conversation. You both know that whatever is shared will be met with empathy and compassion, not judgment. This is crucial for emotional disclosure because it allows you to open up without second-guessing or holding back. In such spaces, honesty flows naturally, fostering a deeper connection.

Creating a safe space requires effort and intention. Key components include active listening without interruption. When your partner speaks, give them your full attention. Let them finish their thoughts without cutting in, even if you want to respond immediately. This patience shows that you value what they're saying. It's not just about hearing words but understanding the emotions behind them. Validating each other's feelings is equally important. Sometimes, just acknowledging your partner's emotions can make all the difference. A simple "I understand why you feel that way" can reassure them that their feelings are valid and important to you.

Maintaining a safe space involves setting clear guidelines to ensure it remains effective for emotional sharing. Establish ground rules for discussions to create a predictable environment where both partners know what to expect. This might involve agreeing to discuss one topic at a time or deciding to table heated discussions until cooler heads prevail. Ensuring confidentiality and privacy is also vital. What's shared in these moments should stay between you unless agreed otherwise. This trust forms the backbone of your safe space, allowing for honest and open exchanges.

The impact of having a safe space in a relationship is profound. It increases emotional security, making both partners feel more comfortable being vulnerable with each other. This security leads to enhanced mutual respect and comfort within the relationship. When both of you know that your thoughts and feelings will be met with understanding, it strengthens your bond and creates a more harmonious partnership. Conversations become more than just exchanges of words; they transform into opportunities for growth and connection.

Incorporating these elements into your relationship requires awareness and commitment from both partners. It's about creating an environment where neither needs to hold back or censor themselves.

Instead, you can engage in meaningful dialogues that deepen your understanding of each other.

Ensuring these safe spaces remain effective over time involves regular check-ins and adjustments as needed. Relationships evolve, and so should the guidelines that support them. Be open to feedback from your partner about what's working well and what might need tweaking. This adaptability ensures that your safe space continues to serve its purpose as both of you navigate new challenges together.

Encouraging emotional disclosure within this supportive framework benefits individual partners and enriches the relationship as a whole. You create a partnership built on trust, respect, and mutual understanding by fostering an atmosphere where openness is celebrated rather than feared.

As you cultivate these safe spaces in your relationship, remember that patience and empathy are key components in maintaining them effectively over time. It may take practice to develop these habits fully. Still, every effort builds a stronger connection between you and your partner.

In the end, safe spaces are about more than just providing a venue for sharing emotions—they're about creating a foundation where both partners feel valued, understood, and empowered to express themselves authentically without fear or hesitation.

Vulnerability Exercises for Couples

Vulnerability exercises aren't just buzzwords; they are gateways to deeper connections. They are structured activities designed to break down walls, providing partners with a safe space to share emotions and thoughts without reservation. These exercises offer opportunities for mutual understanding, allowing both partners to see each other in new, more intimate lights. They aren't about revealing every secret but creating moments where emotional sharing becomes second nature. By practicing these exercises, couples foster an environment where openness flourishes, making it easier to navigate the complexities of a relationship.

Let's dive into some specific exercises you can try. "Emotion sharing" sessions are a great starting point. Set aside time each week to express your feelings—no filters, just raw emotion. It's about saying, "This is where I am right now," and inviting your partner to do the same. Another fun exercise is the "Two truths and a vulnerability" game. In this twist on the classic game, share two truths about your day or week and one vulnerability that made you feel exposed or uncertain. It's a playful yet impactful way to let your partner know what's happening beneath the surface. For something more personal, write letters to each other. Pour your heart out onto the page, then share these letters. It's like handing over a piece of your soul, encouraging intimacy and understanding. These activities aren't just about emotional exposure but about building bridges where gaps once existed.

So, why integrate these exercises into your routine? Regular practice builds a habit of openness, making it second nature to share emotions instead of bottling them up. Over time, these sessions reduce emotional barriers that often lead to misunderstandings or distance.

When you routinely make space for vulnerability, you create a relationship dynamic where true selves are not only welcomed but celebrated. This openness fosters a bond that is both resilient and deeply satisfying.

Approach them with sincerity and openness to get the most out of these exercises. Set a comfortable pace; there's no need to rush through them or force emotions that aren't ready to surface. Encourage patience within yourself and your partner, recognizing that vulnerability can be challenging and doesn't always come easily. Use empathy as your guide, ensuring reactions remain compassionate and understanding rather than judgmental or dismissive.

To execute these exercises effectively, establish a routine that works for both of you. It could be every Sunday evening over a cup of tea or a quiet moment after dinner. The key is consistency—making these practices integral to your relationship rather than sporadic events. Remember to listen as much as you share as you engage in these exercises. Vulnerability is a two-way street; it requires give and take from both partners.

Setting expectations and boundaries beforehand can help create an environment conducive to these exercises. Discuss what each exercise entails and agree on any rules that will help facilitate open communication. For instance, you might decide that during "emotion sharing" sessions, no interruptions are allowed until both have spoken. This ensures that each partner feels heard and valued.

Consider how these exercises can impact your relationship in the long term. As you become more comfortable with vulnerability, conversations will naturally deepen and become more meaningful. You'll start noticing subtle shifts in how you relate to each other—less guardedness, more empathy, and a stronger sense of connection.

Vulnerability exercises are more than just tools for emotional sharing; they're pathways to a richer, more fulfilling partnership. By committing to these practices regularly, you lay the groundwork for a relationship where openness is not just encouraged but thrives. As you continue exploring these exercises together, embrace the journey of discovery and growth they offer, knowing that each step brings you closer to understanding and appreciating each other on a deeper level.

Rebuild Trust After Betrayal

Betrayal in a relationship feels like a sudden storm that leaves chaos in its wake. It can shake the foundation of trust, leaving emotional devastation and a shattered sense of security. When trust is broken, everything feels uncertain. The reliability you once took for granted now seems distant, replaced by doubt and suspicion. It's a raw, painful sensation that can leave both partners questioning the future. This emotional upheaval disrupts the calm you once knew, casting a shadow over what was once a bright and hopeful partnership. For many, the path back to trust feels daunting, yet not impossible.

To rebuild trust, you need to approach it methodically. It starts with an honest acknowledgment of the betrayal. This means owning up to the actions that caused harm without deflecting or making excuses. It requires courage to face the truth head-on and accept the consequences of your actions. Once this acknowledgment is made, commitment to transparency and accountability becomes crucial. Transparency involves being open about your actions and intentions, allowing your partner to see that you're genuinely working towards rebuilding trust. Accountability means consistently following promises and demonstrating reliability in small, everyday actions. These steps lay the groundwork for restoring trust and mending the emotional rift caused by betrayal.

Forgiveness is pivotal in the healing process, though it's often misunderstood. Many think forgiveness means excusing or condoning harmful behavior, but it's more about freeing oneself from resentment. It's a process that takes time and patience, allowing both partners to move forward without the weight of past grievances hanging overhead. Understanding that forgiveness doesn't happen overnight is essential; it's about gradual progress, not perfection. Differentiating forgiveness from condoning actions helps clarify that forgiveness is for personal peace and healing, not justifying wrongdoing. This distinction allows both partners to approach forgiveness with a healthier perspective.

Maintaining trust once it's been rebuilt requires ongoing effort. Consistent follow-through on commitments is essential for demonstrating reliability and reinforcing trustworthiness. This means being dependable in both big and small ways—showing up on time or keeping your word about weekend plans. Open and honest communication channels are equally important for ensuring transparency in your relationship. Regular check-ins can help address any lingering concerns before they become more significant. These practices create an environment where trust can continue to thrive long after the initial rebuilding phase has ended.

As this chapter wraps up, remember that rebuilding trust after betrayal is like tending to a delicate plant. It requires both partners' care, attention, and commitment to nurture growth and healing. While the path may be challenging at times, each step toward restoring trust strengthens the bond between you and your partner, paving the way for a more resilient relationship.

Rebuilding trust after betrayal is a challenging but rewarding journey that demands honesty, transparency, and forgiveness from both partners. It's about acknowledging the hurt caused by betrayal while committing to actions that restore faith in each other over time. As you move forward in this process, remember that maintaining trust requires ongoing effort and dedication, but profound rewards come with perseverance.

In our next chapter, we'll explore strategies for strengthening emotional resilience in your relationship by navigating challenges together with grace and understanding. This exploration will build on the foundation laid here as we continue our journey toward creating a thriving partnership grounded in love and trust.

Chapter Five

Navigate Digital and Traditional Communication

Digital Communication as Friend or Foe

Let's delve deeper into this modern conundrum. You are meticulously composing a quick text message to your partner, filled with love and excitement about the evening's dinner plans. However, your partner misinterprets the message's intention or emotional undertone due to the absence of a vocal tone or non-verbal communication. What was meant to be a sweet interaction suddenly spirals into a wave of miscommunication as they text back, seeking clarification: "What did you mean by that?" This perfectly illustrates the double-edged nature of digital communication. It brings us the unparalleled convenience of maintaining connections despite vast distances yet at the same time poses challenges that can strain relational dynamics.

On one hand, digital communication is undeniably a newfound boon in maintaining relationships over considerable distances. The lifeline that instant messaging provides allows for genuine, swift interactions. You can share the fleeting moments of your daily life—a delightful sunrise captured on your phone or a quick thought that made you laugh. It is a tool that enables you to send affectionate messages or share heartfelt sentiments when physical presence is not an option. The lack of geographical limitations means you can remain an integral part of your loved one's life, nurturing the bond as you exchange pictures, videos, and real-time anecdotes—a glue that keeps relationships sturdy when spending time together in person isn't possible.

Nevertheless, the pitfalls of digital communication must be acknowledged. Consider the scenario where you are trying to have a meaningful discussion with your partner in person. Yet, their attention is diverted to a buzzing phone screen at every turn. That small device overshadows your significant presence, making you feel secondary to digital distractions. According to the comprehensive data compiled by the Pew Research Center, a reputable institution known for its research on social issues, 40% of individuals in committed relationships report feeling annoyed by their partner's phone usage during critical face-to-face conversations, highlighting a common grievance (Dating and Relationships in the Digital Age). Furthermore, the absence of context in digital exchanges can lead to compounding misunderstandings. Messages composed hastily or void of fundamental context can spiral into a breeding ground of confusion and frustration.

Navigating this digital labyrinth requires intentional strategies and mindfulness. Initially, assess how digital interactions feature in your relationship. Reflect on both your and your partner's digital habits. Are you more inclined to text than speak directly? Initiate a conversation with your partner about setting intentional, mutually agreed boundaries for using digital devices, especially during quality time together. For instance, you could keep phones away during meals or dedicate specific time blocks to unplugging from electronic distractions. In doing so, you prioritize face-to-face communication, ensuring that digital channels serve as an enhancement rather than a hindrance to your relationship.

An effective strategy for evaluating your digital habits is cultivating self-awareness through a straightforward checklist. Note how frequently you check your mobile device during interpersonal interactions or assess how often substantial conversations are reduced to mere text exchanges. This practice fosters mindfulness, enabling both of you to identify patterns that may benefit from recalibration. It is about fostering equilibrium—harmonizing the act of staying continuously connected with the essential practice of being present and fully engaged.

By emphasizing the importance of balance in digital communication, the audience can feel empowered and in control. Digital communication, much like any tool, is neither intrinsically beneficial nor detrimental; its value lies in how we harness its potential. Acknowledging its dual facets, you can use digital advancements to fortify your relationship while consciously mitigating its challenges. By weaving together the strengths of digital and traditional communication methods, you can forge an adaptive and symbiotic blend that perfectly aligns with your distinct relationship dynamic. Embrace its advantages while remaining vigilant of its limitations, paving the way for a cohesive and enriched communication experience.

Strategies for a Healthy Digital Detox

Emphasizing the benefits of a digital detox can instill a sense of hope and motivation in the audience. It's about stepping back from the screens often dominating our lives and reconnecting with the present. This pause can help reduce dependency on technology, allowing you to focus more on each other. Imagine entirely conversing without glancing at your phone every few minutes. It's about savoring the moment, being truly present, and rediscovering the joy of uninterrupted connection. A digital detox doesn't mean abandoning technology altogether; it's about finding balance and ensuring that tech serves your relationship, not the other way around.

Some signs indicate that you and your partner need a digital detox. Have you noticed an almost reflexive habit of checking your phone during conversations? Or maybe there's an underlying anxiety when you can't access your device right away. These behaviors suggest that your reliance on technology might be overshadowing real-life interactions. Feeling anxious without your phone is common, but it can become problematic when it interferes with quality time together. Consider a detox if your partner seems more absorbed in their screen than in your stories. It's about recognizing when technology takes precedence over personal connections.

How do you go about implementing a digital detox without disrupting daily life? Start by designating tech-free zones in your home. The dining table could be one space where phones and tablets are off-limits, encouraging conversation during meals. Scheduling regular "unplugged" hours is another effective strategy. Choose times when both of you agree to put devices aside and focus solely on each other. This could be during breakfast or an hour before bed. Engaging in tech-free activities together can also help reinforce the detox. Consider going for walks, cooking, or playing board games—anything that fosters interaction without screens.

The benefits of a successful detox are well worth the effort. You'll likely find more face-to-face interaction, leading to richer and more meaningful conversations. Without digital interruptions, you can truly listen and engage with one another, deepening your connection. Enhanced mindfulness and focus are other positive outcomes. By reducing screen time, you're more attuned to each other's needs and emotions, fostering a sense of harmony and understanding. This mindfulness extends beyond just interactions with each other; it permeates daily life, helping you appreciate the small moments often overlooked when distracted by devices.

Assessing Your Digital Habits

Encouraging the audience to assess their digital habits can make them feel introspective and self-aware. Take a moment to reflect on your digital habits. How often do you check your phone during conversations with your partner? Do you reach for it out of habit or necessity? Write down your observations and discuss them with your partner. This exercise can help you become more aware of how technology impacts your relationship and guide you in setting boundaries.

A digital detox isn't a one-time fix; it's about crafting sustainable habits that promote healthier communication patterns. It requires commitment from both partners to prioritize each other over screens, creating a shared understanding of what matters most in your relationship. You're taking steps toward a more fulfilling connection by setting clear boundaries and consciously engaging more deeply with each other.

In our fast-paced world, it's easy for technology to overshadow personal interactions. But by embracing a digital detox, you're choosing to refocus on what truly matters—each other. It's about making intentional choices that foster love, understanding, and connection. Remember that small changes can significantly improve how you relate to one another.

Maintain Connection Across Distances

Long-distance relationships often feel like a never-ending waiting game. You're not counting down the days until the next visit but also juggling time zone differences that transform simple exchanges into logistical challenges. For instance, imagine the thrill of your promotion being dashed by the sobering realization that your partner is merely starting their day halfway across the globe. These time zone mismatches necessitate deeper strategic planning, making even a casual conversation similar to solving a jigsaw puzzle. The lack of spontaneous chats transforms a seamless interaction into a predetermined bout of exchanges.

Additionally, the undeniable limitation is posed by the absence of a physical presence. The comforting hug or the shared burst of laughter over dinner, staples of close-knit relationships, are conspicuously absent. This absence tends to amplify feelings of loneliness, intensifying your yearning for the simple, albeit powerful, touch or a glance that conveys volumes without saying a single word.

Staying connected when miles apart demands creativity, commitment, and an unwavering dedication to nurturing what you have through unconventional means. Regular video call dates evolve into your lifeline, providing invaluable glimpses into each other's daily lives, even if it's simply sharing a breakfast brew through a screen. These aren't just technological marvels; they're precious moments where you bridge the vast distance with eye contact that can speak more than conversation and shared smiles that can brighten the dullest days. Engaging in virtual shared activities, like immersing yourselves in online games, becomes a playful reprieve, morphing routine screen time into a delightful playtime that refreshes and rejuvenates both spirits. Let us also embrace the endearing charm of retro communication methods. Sending care packages or crafting handwritten letters revives nostalgia. Imagine the impact of a surprise package, filled to the brim with favorite snacks or intricately written heartfelt notes; such gestures pack an emotional punch, echoing sentiments of love and reminding your partner of their cherished place in your heart.

Technology, wielded with skill and sensibility, is a formidable ally in bridging these chasms. Collaborative apps for shared tasks transcend mundane activities into cooperative endeavors, transforming a potential monotony into an engaging partnership. Whether planning a dream vacation or managing a digital grocery list, these apps cultivate a sense of togetherness. With the advent of online streaming services, watching shows together becomes a tapestry of shared delight, syncing your laughter and reacting parallel to each other, even when oceans apart. These seemingly small acts weave the tapestry of your relationship together, creating shared experiences that solidify your bond despite the vast divide.

While technology plays a crucial role, planning for in-person visits remains an unwavering pillar of such relationships. The anticipation of seeing each other ignites sparks in your daily existence, giving you both a tangible joy to look forward to. It requires meticulous coordination and patience beyond measure to ensure regular meet-ups, but these are indispensable for sustaining intimacy. Crafting detailed itineraries for these precious visits ensures every moment is savored and valued, whether exploring new locales or simply basking in each other's tranquil company. These interactions reinforce your bond's steadfast resilience, reminding both parties why they remain steadfast in their commitment to making it work, defying distance and skepticism.

Though laden with challenges that test your resiliency and creativity, long-distance relationships can deepen mutual understanding and reinforce commitment. They compel you to hone your skills in intentional communication, elevating each word and gesture to carry meaningful weight. As you chart these waters of adversity, always remember that every conscious effort you channel into staying connected acts as a bridge, drawing you nearer to one another regardless of the countless miles that might lie between.

Digital Etiquette for Couples

Navigating our digital interactions requires a certain finesse. This delicate balance can often feel as elusive as a whisper in the wind. This is where digital etiquette comes into play, a term that encapsulates the unspoken rules of conduct in our online lives. Think of it as the virtual equivalent of saying "please" and "thank you," fundamental courtesies that smoothen our interactions with those we hold dear. In essence, digital etiquette is about maintaining respect and consideration throughout our virtual communications, ensuring that the integrity of our relationships remains intact even in the digital sphere.

Imagine your partner sharing something deeply personal with you — a cherished memory or a sensitive secret — and suddenly, without their consent, it's out there for the world to see. This lapse in judgment can strain trust, as respecting privacy and boundaries is paramount in any healthy relationship. We must learn to differentiate between what is appropriate to share with the world and what should remain confined to the intimate bubble of the relationship. Furthermore, avoiding public disagreements on social media is another critical component of digital etiquette. After all, who would relish publicly having relationship issues aired for everyone to witness and comment on? It's much like airing dirty laundry, creating a spectacle rather than maintaining the dignity such matters truly deserve. Consequently, it becomes vital to handle conflicts privately, upholding the sanctity of your relationship.

Sometimes, in our fast-paced digital lives, we inadvertently slip into behaviors that breach digital etiquette, ultimately causing harm to our relationships. For example, ignoring messages or calls from your partner can unintentionally convey a disheartening message of indifference or neglect. Picture it like walking past someone trying to speak to you without a nod or a glance of acknowledgment. This seemingly minor action can sow seeds of doubt and insecurity over time. Similarly, there is the delicate matter of over-sharing personal details without your partner's consent. Such errant actions can make your partner feel exposed, vulnerable, or betrayed. Though these indiscretions may seem minor in isolation, collectively, they can cause significant damage, eroding trust and creating challenging rifts.

To practice good digital etiquette, start by setting clear expectations for response times with your partner. The goal is not about being perpetually glued to your phone but about ensuring your partner knows when to expect a response, averting any unnecessary anxiety or misunderstandings. Discuss social media boundaries to jointly decide what content is appropriate to share and what should remain private. This proactive conversation prevents misunderstandings and safeguards each other's privacy, thus fortifying your relationship against potential digital breaches. Furthermore, make a conscious effort to use respectful language in digital and face-to-face communication. Since tone can be easily misinterpreted in text-based conversations, carefully choosing your words can help circumvent unnecessary conflicts or misunderstandings that could escalate.

Good digital etiquette can significantly impact relationship health by cultivating a sense of trust and respect. When both partners commit to adhering to these guidelines, it minimizes digital misunderstandings and discourages unnecessary arguments. It's akin to laying down a solid foundation of mutual respect, where both partners feel valued, cherished, and understood. Trust flourishes when you know your partner respects your online and offline boundaries. This trust, in turn, enhances communication, allowing the relationship to bloom without the constant looming fear of digital missteps eroding the intimacy you've worked hard to build.

Building a relationship in today's digital world involves a nuanced understanding of how our online actions impact those we love. Imagine if every text message or social media post was crafted with the same meticulous care and heartfelt sincerity as a handwritten letter. Digital etiquette creates a safe, respectful space where love can thrive uninhibited in the digital age. When approached thoughtfully, it fosters an environment that supports emotional intimacy, ensuring that both partners can navigate the ever-evolving digital communication landscape with grace, respect, and unwavering love.

Blend Digital and In-Person Communication

Balancing digital and in-person communication can feel like juggling multiple balls in the air, each representing a different aspect of your relationship. It's about finding that sweet spot where technology enhances and doesn't overshadow your time together. Consider using digital tools to organize your face-to-face meetups. Consider a shared calendar app to schedule date nights or reminders for important anniversaries. This tech-savvy approach ensures you're both on the same page, reducing the likelihood of missed plans or forgotten commitments. Planning in advance lets you focus on enjoying your time together without the stress of last-minute arrangements.

Transitioning between online and offline interactions requires finesse. Think of it like shifting gears in a car, where each transition needs to be smooth to maintain the overall flow. Begin with a digital conversation that naturally leads into an in-person discussion. For instance, if you're texting about a new show you've both started watching, why not plan to watch the next episode together? This approach keeps the conversation alive and creates shared experiences that strengthen your bond. Use digital reminders to ensure that both of you remember these plans, preventing potential hiccups.

The beauty of blending these forms of communication lies in the comprehensive understanding it fosters. When you effectively balance digital and personal interactions, you gain a deeper insight into your partner's needs and preferences. It's like having a well-rounded view that captures both the nuances of their texts and the subtleties of their expressions during face-to-face chats. This natural approach enhances flexibility and adaptability, allowing you to adjust your communication style based on context. You'll find that your relationship becomes more resilient and capable of weathering challenges that might have previously caused friction.

However, achieving this balance isn't always smooth sailing. Digital distractions can sneak in during personal time, pulling focus away from meaningful interactions. It's all too easy to get lost in a sea of notifications and social media updates when you should be engaging with each other. To counter this, consider setting guidelines for device use during quality time. Maybe agree on specific "no phone" zones or times when both commit to being fully present. This creates a space where your attention is solely on each other, fostering deeper connections.

Another challenge is maintaining momentum when transitioning from digital to face-to-face conversations. Online exchanges sometimes feel less personal, making it tricky to maintain the same level of engagement in person. One solution is to build anticipation for your meetups through digital interactions. Share snippets of your day or send playful messages that spark curiosity, creating excitement when you finally get together.

In summary, blending digital and in-person communication allows you to enjoy the best of both worlds. It's about using technology to enrich your relationship while ensuring it doesn't overshadow the genuine connection from being together in person. By finding the right balance, you create a dynamic where both forms of communication complement each other, leading to a more fulfilling partnership.

Remember that integrating digital and traditional communication is ongoing. Both partners require mindfulness and intentionality to ensure that technology serves as an enhancement rather than a hindrance. Moving into the next chapter, we'll explore creating lasting love by building trust and understanding through effective communication strategies. Together, we'll continue our exploration of ways to deepen your connection and strengthen your bond for the long haul.

Chapter Six

Customize Communication Styles for Compatibility

Discover Your Communication Style

Think of the discord at a dinner table where you and your partner speak different languages. The barriers aren't due to a lack of understanding in a linguistic sense but rather the friction from mismatched communication styles echoing like clashing cymbals at a grand concert. This scenario illustrates the pivotal role of understanding your unique communication style, acting as a navigator's tool through the complex maze of daily interactions. It operates as a personal roadmap, helping you articulate thoughts and emotions without being mangled into misunderstandings or lost in translation.

Communication style assessments serve as your compass in this journey, providing insights into your habitual conversational patterns and how they potentially harmonize or discord with your partner's. By exploring models such as "The Four Communication Styles" or the Myers-Briggs Type Indicator (MBTI), you unearth nuances about your inclinations—whether towards assertiveness, marked by clear and direct expression, or a passive demeanor that perhaps shuns confrontation in favor of harmony. These revelations are transformative, converting what might have been battlegrounds of misunderstandings into fertile grounds for connection and understanding.

For couples embarking on this enlightening discovery, the journey begins with engaging in joint communication style quizzes. These exercises verify individual traits and pinpoint areas for mutual enhancement. It's a reflective mirror, highlighting where strengths and growth opportunities lie. A step further involves reflecting on past conversations and dissecting them for recurring patterns—in disagreements or expressions of affection. This insight shows whether you naturally sway towards assertiveness's upfront nature or the peace-preserving tendencies of passiveness.

Understanding different communication characteristics plays a significant role in relationship dynamics. Assertive communicators, like a lighthouse, illuminate interactions with clarity and purpose, emphasizing honesty and mutual respect. Conversely, passive communicators shy away from conflict, often prioritizing peace and harmony over their immediate needs, the same as peacekeepers maintaining calm in tumultuous seas. Recognizing these traits helps you understand the undercurrents shaping your interactions, revealing how varying styles can pave the way for potential misinterpretations—for instance, when an assertive partner's forthrightness might overwhelm a more reserved, passive one.

Yet, within these differences lies a pond of potential harmony and growth. Assertive partners can uplift their quieter counterparts, encouraging them to voice opinions with greater confidence and certainty. For instance, they can create a safe space for their partner to express their thoughts without fear of judgment. In turn, passive partners lend lessons in patience and empathy, softening the edges of assertiveness into understated harmony.

Working through these intricate dynamics often demands adaptability and patience. It is paramount to acknowledge that communication is not a one-size-fits-all affair but rather a tailor-made experience. Much like finely tuning instruments in a grand orchestra, adaptability in communication styles can lead to a symphony of harmony and understanding within the relationship.

Charting Your Communication Terrain

Take a moment to look back at yourself by grabbing a notebook to pen down recent exchanges with your partner. What patterns spring forth? Identify themes, both resonant and discordant, in how you converse. Use this reflection as a compass to chart your unique communication terrain, spotlighting junctures where styles synchronously align or diverge.

Remember that discovering your communication style isn't about confining yourself within rigid boundaries but rather attaining a deep-rooted understanding of how to forge connections most effectively. Consider it a personalized guidebook for your relationship, filled with insights for navigating conversations with newfound empathy and robust understanding.

Embracing this knowledge empowers couples to cultivate deeper connections and joyful, fulfilling interactions. Whether you lean towards assertiveness or passiveness, understanding your style enables engagement with intention and clarity. It's about forging a nurturing environment where both partners feel acknowledged, heard, and cherished—building bridges of understanding through the nuanced art of communication.

Thus, understanding communication styles is a tool and a gateway to elevating relational dynamics. It empowers couples to bridge divides and anchor common ground, turning potential conflicts into springboards for growth and deeper connection. By embarking on this exploration together, partners can cultivate an environment where understanding thrives, and love flourishes to its fullest potential.

Align Differing Communication Styles for Better Interaction

The friction that often arises between differing communication styles can be compared to two dancers trying to perform a duet while listening to entirely different music. Imagine one partner living in a world of assertive clarity, firing off thoughts directly and expecting immediate responses. At the same time, the other prefers a calmer, more contemplative approach, taking time to process and reflect before speaking. This misalignment can lead to misinterpretations and frustration. Intentions get lost in translation, and what was meant as a straightforward comment spirals into a misunderstanding. You might feel like speaking clearly, but your partner hears something entirely different.

It's crucial to establish a common ground to navigate and align these differing styles. This isn't about changing who you are but finding shared spaces in communication where both feel understood. Start with small agreements on how to communicate effectively. You can agree on specific discussion times, ensuring neither is caught off guard or unprepared. Create joint communication goals, like improving listening skills or reducing interruptions. These goals become anchors in daily interactions, providing stability and direction.

Compromise plays a fundamental role in this alignment process. It is the bridge connecting divergent styles, allowing both partners to meet halfway. In communication styles, compromise means finding a balance between assertiveness and receptivity. It's about knowing when to push for clarity and when to lean back and give space for reflection. Balancing these elements requires patience and a willingness to adapt. Perhaps during a discussion, you agree to pause before responding, giving the more reflective partner time to gather their thoughts without feeling rushed.

Aligned communication leads to smoother interactions and satisfying dialogues. It creates a rhythm where conversations flow naturally without the usual bumps and halts that come with misalignment. When you synchronize your styles, mutual understanding improves significantly. You anticipate each other's needs, reducing the chances of conflict born from simple miscommunications. The emotional connection between you deepens as well because aligned communication fosters an environment where both partners feel heard and valued.

Developing aligned communication is like learning to dance together—each step must be taken with awareness and intention. Couples can create a harmonious interaction pattern that honors both individuals' preferences by focusing on finding common ground and negotiating boundaries. This doesn't mean erasing differences but celebrating them in ways that enhance connection rather than hinder it.

Communication Style Mapping

Take some time to map out typical conversations with your partner. Identify areas where styles diverge. This process, known as 'communication style mapping,' can help you visualize your communication patterns and understand where misalignments occur. Use this map as a guide to pinpoint where compromise might be needed, creating a visual tool that highlights potential areas for alignment. By doing so, you can proactively address these areas and work towards a more harmonious communication style.

The benefits of aligning your communication styles extend beyond just reducing misunderstandings. As you align more closely, you lay the groundwork for a relationship marked by respect and empathy. Conversations become opportunities to connect rather than minefields to navigate cautiously. Each partner learns to appreciate the other's style, transforming differences into complementary strengths that enrich the relationship.

Aligning communication styles isn't a one-time fix but an ongoing process requiring effort and openness from both partners. It demands an understanding that effective communication is a shared responsibility—a dance performed together rather than solo efforts made in parallel. By embracing this approach, you open the door to deeper connection and understanding, paving the way for a more fulfilling relationship.

In your search to align communication styles for better interaction, remember that every step taken towards understanding your partner's unique voice brings you closer to a harmonious relationship where both feel acknowledged and cherished. The path may have challenges, but the rewards of improved dialogue and emotional connection make it an endeavor worth pursuing. So take that step, tune in to each other's rhythm, and let your conversations unfold like a beautifully choreographed dance where both partners move together in perfect harmony.

Overcome Misaligned Communication

Ever feel like you're speaking to your partner, but the words seem to bounce off like you're not on the same wavelength? That's a classic sign of misaligned communication. It's that moment when you're sharing something important, and instead of feeling connected, there's a disconnect or a misunderstanding. You might walk away from a chat feeling like you spoke different languages. Misalignment can sneak up in frequent misunderstandings where intentions don't match interpretations. One partner might think they're being clear, while the other is left trying to decode the message. This misalignment often leads to emotional disconnects during conversations, where neither feels genuinely heard or understood.

When communication styles clash, it can ripple through your relationship like a misplaced chord in a beautiful symphony. This misalignment often breeds increased tension and frustration. Arguments can erupt over seemingly trivial matters because beneath the surface lies a sea of unresolved friction. Emotional withdrawal might follow, where partners retreat into their shells rather than risk another misstep. This creates a vicious cycle where both parties feel isolated, exacerbating feelings of loneliness even in each other's company. It's easy to see how misalignment can chip away at the foundation of trust and intimacy, leaving both partners adrift.

So, how do you bridge this gap and realign your styles? Start by adjusting your tone and language to better suit your partner's preferences. Like tuning an instrument to harmonize with a band, it's about finding that sweet spot where your words resonate rather than jar. Regular feedback sessions can be invaluable here. Set aside time to discuss what's working and what isn't in your communication. These sessions aren't about pointing fingers; they're about tuning into each other's needs and making adjustments as necessary. Practicing empathy is another crucial step. Put yourself in your partner's shoes and try to see things from their perspective. This doesn't mean agreeing with everything they say but acknowledging their viewpoint as valid and worthy of consideration.

Consider exploring tools that encourage ongoing communication growth to maintain this newfound alignment. Attend workshops or seminars on communication techniques where you can learn new strategies together. Relationship coaching offers tailored guidance for aligning communication styles, giving you personalized feedback and strategies to improve interaction. These resources provide structured environments where you can develop skills in a supportive setting, offering new insights into each other's communication needs.

Think of these efforts as tending to a garden. Regular attention and care help maintain a vibrant relationship where both partners feel seen and heard. Communication workshops act as the sunlight, nurturing growth and understanding, while feedback sessions are like pruning—removing what doesn't work to make way for healthier interactions. Relationship coaching offers the tools to cultivate and sustain harmony, ensuring that misalignments don't take root and disrupt your connection.

Achieving alignment requires both partners to continually assess and adapt their communication styles. It's not about changing who you are but instead finding ways to connect more effectively with each other. Focusing on these solutions creates an environment where communication flows smoothly, fostering deeper emotional connections and reducing misunderstandings.

While working through your styles to overcome misaligned communication, remember that every effort made toward understanding your partner's unique voice brings you closer to a relationship anchored in mutual respect and empathy. The journey may have its challenges, but the rewards of improved dialogue and connection make it a task worth pursuing. So take that leap, tune in to each other's rhythm, and let your conversations unfold with renewed clarity and understanding—one step at a time.

Tailor Communication to Meet Individual Needs

Think of trying to solve a puzzle with pieces that don't quite fit together. That's what communication in relationships can feel like when it's not tailored to the individual needs of each partner. Recognizing that one size doesn't fit all in communication is crucial. Each person brings unique preferences, perspectives, and emotional landscapes. Acknowledging these personal preferences isn't just kind; it's necessary for cultivating a satisfying and supportive relationship. When you engage with your partner in a way that resonates with their personal style, you enhance emotional support and create a sense of safety and belonging.

To understand these individual needs, begin by crafting a "needs inventory" list. This isn't a one-time activity; it's an ongoing process. Sit down with your partner and talk about what you both need from each other to feel heard and valued. What makes you feel supported during tough conversations? What words or phrases resonate with you? What words or phrases trigger high emotional feelings? Discussing personal communication boundaries is a significant step. Boundaries aren't walls to keep each other out but guidelines that show how to engage meaningfully without stepping on toes. Knowing these boundaries helps you communicate in a way that feels comfortable and respectful.

Once you've identified these needs, it's time to put them into practice. Adapting your language to match your partner's comfort level is powerful. It's not about changing who you are but communicating naturally for both of you. Depending on your partner's preferences, this might mean using more affirming language or being more direct. Scheduling regular check-ins is another excellent strategy to address evolving needs. Relationships aren't static, and neither are the people in them. By making time for regular conversations about how things are going, you stay attuned to each other's changing needs and can adjust your communication accordingly.

The benefits of personalized communication are profound. When you tailor your interactions to meet individual needs, you foster stronger bonds built on mutual respect. Increased relationship satisfaction is one of the first things you'll notice. There's something profoundly fulfilling about feeling genuinely understood by your partner. Emotional fulfillment follows naturally as well. When both partners feel seen and heard, it paves the way for a deeper emotional connection that enriches the overall relationship experience.

Personalized communication isn't just about avoiding misunderstandings but creating a rich tapestry of shared experiences where both partners feel valued and understood. This approach transforms everyday interactions from routine exchanges into meaningful dialogues that strengthen your connection. It's about recognizing that your partner's needs matter as much as yours and consciously meeting them with empathy and understanding.

Adopting this mindset requires ongoing effort and commitment from both partners. It's about regularly revisiting those "needs inventory" lists and checking with each other about how things are going. It's about recognizing that communication is an ever-evolving dance where both partners take turns leading and following based on their unique rhythms.

Bringing these strategies into your daily interactions can transform how you relate to each other, fostering an environment where love and understanding flourish. By tailoring communication to meet individual needs, you create a partnership where both feel cherished and supported—a relationship that survives and thrives amidst life's challenges.

Remember that personalized communication is not about changing who you are but enhancing how you connect. It's about embracing your partner's unique needs while honoring your own, creating a harmonious balance where both voices are heard and valued equally.

So take that step toward tailoring communication in your relationship today, knowing that every effort to understand your partner's unique voice brings you closer to a fulfilling connection filled with empathy, respect, and love.

Effective Techniques for Diverse Dynamics

Picture a mosaic, each tile representing a unique relationship dynamic. Non-traditional relationships and cross-cultural couples add vibrant colors and patterns to this mosaic, enriching the tapestry of human connection. These diverse dynamics bring unique challenges in communication but also offer tremendous opportunities for growth and understanding. In non-traditional relationships, clear communication is the lifeline that connects multiple partners while honoring individual bonds. Cross-cultural couples often navigate the nuances of different traditions and values, blending them into a harmonious relationship symphony. Recognizing these diverse structures helps tailor communication techniques that meet each relationship's needs.

Adapting communication styles for cultural sensitivity is crucial to communicate in these diverse dynamics. This means understanding and respecting cultural nuances influencing how partners perceive and express emotions. For instance, in some cultures, openly expressing emotions is encouraged, while in others, subtlety is valued. By being mindful of these differences, you avoid missteps that might lead to misunderstandings. Using inclusive language also plays a significant role. Language that respects relationship diversity acknowledges and validates love's various forms. It's about saying "partner" instead of assuming "husband" or "wife," thus creating an environment where all feel seen and respected.

Collaborating on communication strategies honors each partner's background, weaving their stories into a shared narrative. This requires open discussions about what each partner values in communication and finding ways to incorporate those elements into daily interactions. It's about creating a relationship blueprint that integrates the best of both worlds, whether combining traditional practices with modern approaches or finding common ground in differing belief systems.

Emphasizing inclusivity in communication practices fosters an environment where each partner feels valued for their unique perspective. Recognizing and validating different viewpoints strengthens the bond between partners, turning diversity into a relationship strength rather than a challenge. Celebrating diversity means appreciating how differing backgrounds enrich the relationship with broader perspectives and more profound empathy. It's about cultivating an environment where differences are tolerated and cherished for the richness they bring to the partnership.

Effective communication within diverse dynamics enhances relationship resilience and understanding. When partners embrace their differences, they become more adaptable, learning to navigate life's challenges flexibly and gracefully. This adaptability stems from continually adjusting communication styles to meet evolving needs and circumstances. Moreover, diverse dynamics offer enriched relational experiences. They expose partners to new ideas and ways of thinking, fostering a culture of lifelong learning within the relationship. Each interaction becomes an opportunity to learn something new about each other and the world around them.

In summary, embracing diversity in relationships transforms potential communication hurdles into stepping stones for growth and connection. By adapting communication styles for cultural sensitivity, using inclusive language, and celebrating diversity as a strength, couples can build resilient relationships that thrive amidst life's challenges. The techniques discussed here serve as tools for fostering understanding and empathy in diverse dynamics, ensuring that every partner feels heard and valued.

In closing this chapter on customizing communication styles for compatibility, remember that each relationship is as unique as its people. Embracing this uniqueness through tailored communication enriches your connection with your partner, paving the way for a fulfilling relationship grounded in mutual respect and understanding. In the next chapter, we'll explore how to strengthen emotional bonds by integrating empathy and emotional intelligence into your everyday interactions—an essential step towards further deepening your connection with your partner.

Chapter Seven

Practical Exercises for Lasting Change

Active Listening Exercises for Daily Practice

You're sitting across from your partner at the comforting confines of the kitchen table. Each of you has a warm cup of coffee in hand, the aroma drifting through the air, contributing to an atmosphere ripe for meaningful connection. Here, amidst the soft clinks of coffee cups and comfortable seats, is where active listening takes center stage. This is not merely a practice of nodding passively as your partner speaks; it is an engaged endeavor where you dive into their words, endeavoring to grasp the nuances of their perspective while crafting thoughtful responses that reflect a deep understanding.

Active listening workshops are not just transformative; they are platforms that can significantly hone these invaluable skills. Whether through one-on-one interactions or in a group setting, these workshops offer a structured approach to a weekly tune-up for both your ears and heart. They transform how you engage, empathize, and connect daily with those you care about.

Consider dedicating specific time slots for weekly sessions to enhance your journey into active listening. These sessions are not designed to be mere casual chatter but represent moments set apart for the mindful practicing of intentional listening. During these valuable sessions, delve into interactive listening games designed to make the process enjoyable and insightful. Picture a scenario where you and your partner alternate speaking on a chosen topic for a set duration of, say, five minutes, as the other listens intently without interjecting. Afterward, exchange thoughts on what was heard, reflecting on content and emotional impact. Through this playful approach, monotony is disrupted. It reinforces the importance of fully engaging and being present in every conversation you share.

Adding daily listening exercises into your routine is key to locking these newfound skills in place. One simple yet effective practice is the 'Repeat and Reflect' exercise. Once your partner shares their thoughts, take a moment to paraphrase their message. For instance, if they express work-related stress, you might mirror this by saying, 'It sounds like your workload is overwhelming right now.' This technique ensures clarity and mutual understanding, helping to eradicate the potential for miscommunication in your daily conversations.

Maintaining a ' listening journal ' is another valuable tool in your active listening repertoire. In this journal, document daily instances where you actively practiced listening, reflecting on the insights and learning derived from these interactions. This documentation is a tangible record of your progress, highlighting achievements and areas ripe for further development.

The profound impact of steadfast active listening practice is unmistakable. As tuning in to your partner's emotional landscape becomes second nature, a heightened emotional connection blossoms, strengthening your intimate bond. Misunderstandings dwindle, replaced by a new standard where both partners feel deeply heard and genuinely understood. This clarity fuels a harmonious relationship where conflicts find smoother resolution and communication flows effortlessly like a well-tuned symphony.

To further enable this transformation, consider setting explicit listening goals. You may aim to interrupt less frequently, honing your ability to paraphrase accurately. Illustrate these goals by creating a progress chart and celebrating milestones achieved along the way. This visual representation is an encouraging reminder of your journey's advancement, fostering motivation for continued growth in expanding your listening skills.

By weaving active listening into the very fabric of your relationship, you go beyond merely hearing spoken words—a profound connection emerges on a deeper level. Through this practice, conversations shift from routine exchanges to invaluable opportunities for growth, mutual understanding, and nurturing the rich bonds between you and your partner.

Empathy-Building Activities for Couples

There's a room buzzing with quiet anticipation as couples gather for an empathy-building workshop. The atmosphere is supportive, inviting each participant to explore the depths of their partner's emotions. These workshops are designed to foster understanding and compassion, offering a structured environment where you can learn to see the world through your partner's eyes. Interactive group sessions allow couples to share experiences and learn from each other, creating a communal space where empathy becomes second nature. These activities' sense of unity and shared growth will make you feel connected and supported in your empathy-building journey.

One powerful exercise at home is the "Walk in My Shoes" role reversal. Swap roles with your partner and act out a familiar scenario from their perspective. Whether handling morning chaos or navigating a demanding workday, this exercise offers insight into each other's daily challenges and emotions. It's a simple concept, yet it opens doors to empathy that might have been closed. Another activity is the "Emotion Exploration" session. Set aside time to talk openly about feelings—no judgments, just understanding. Discuss what made you happy or upset during the week and why it mattered. These conversations deepen your emotional connection, paving the way for more compassionate interactions.

Empathy exercises aren't just about understanding each other better; they're about strengthening the fabric of your relationship. When you engage in these activities, you cultivate emotional empathy—an ability to connect on a level that is more than mere words. This empathy enhances relationship satisfaction, as both partners feel seen and valued. The bond between you grows stronger, rooted in mutual understanding and respect.

Let's discuss how to personalize these exercises for your unique relationship dynamics. Start by considering your comfort levels. If role-playing feels too intense, begin with simpler activities like shared storytelling or discussing past experiences. Tailor exercises to reflect your cultural backgrounds or personal histories, incorporating elements that resonate deeply with both of you. This personalization makes the exercises more meaningful and relevant to your life, making you feel understood and respected in your relationship.

For example, imagine a couple where one partner grew up in a culture that emphasizes community and collective well-being, while the other comes from a background valuing individual achievement. In their empathy-building sessions, they might share stories from their childhoods that highlight these cultural differences, helping each understand the other's perspective more fully. By adjusting exercises in this way, you not only enrich the experience but also foster a deeper appreciation for what makes each partner unique.

Empathy-building workshops and exercises are not just tools but gateways to a richer, more fulfilling relationship. They invite you into a world where understanding and kindness are at the forefront, transforming how you relate to each other daily. Through these activities, you learn to navigate the complexities of emotions with grace and patience, ensuring that your connection remains strong and resilient.

Remember that empathy is a skill that grows with practice. It requires openness and a willingness to be vulnerable, yet the rewards are numerous. Investing time in these activities lays the groundwork for a relationship built on mutual respect and compassion.

Imagine sharing these exercises with friends or family members who might benefit from them. Empathy is contagious; as you cultivate it within your relationship, its effects ripple outward, enriching your interactions beyond just your partnership.

Conflict Resolution Role-Playing Scenarios

Imagine stepping into a scene where you and your partner are actors, improvising through a typical conflict. Role-playing for conflict resolution offers a safe stage to practice resolving disputes. It allows you to rehearse reactions and solutions in a controlled environment. You can see how different approaches play out without the stakes of real-life consequences. Think of it as a rehearsal before the main performance, where you get to understand each other's perspectives more deeply. By simulating scenarios, you become more adept at navigating conflicts when they arise.

Let's play a common scenario: "Miscommunication at dinner." You both come home exhausted, hoping for a relaxing meal. But something gets lost in translation. Maybe one of you expected takeout while the other cooked, leading to frustration. In this role-play, take turns playing each other's roles. Express how your partner might feel and watch them mirror your feelings. This builds empathy and provides insights into how you both perceive situations differently. Another scenario could be "Balancing work and home responsibilities," where the pressure of juggling tasks leads to friction. By acting out these situations, you can explore solutions together, trying different strategies in a low-pressure setting.

The benefits of role-playing are numerous. For starters, it boosts your confidence in handling factual disputes. When you've already worked through a problem in practice, facing it in reality feels less daunting. Plus, role-playing enhances problem-solving skills by encouraging creativity and collaboration. You learn to think on your feet and adapt, skills that are invaluable when unexpected issues arise. Through this method, you and your partner become a team, working together to refine your conflict resolution toolkit.

After each role-play session, it's crucial to review. This reflection helps solidify what you've learned and identify areas for improvement. Sit down together and discuss what worked well and what could be tweaked. One approach resonated more than another, or maybe there was an aha moment that clarified a recurring issue. Journaling these insights can be particularly beneficial. Write down your thoughts after each session, documenting progress and noting any emerging patterns. This practice encourages continuous learning and growth.

Review Sessions

Create a structured review session after role-playing exercises. Allocate time for each partner to share their perspective on the exercise—what they learned, what surprised them, and what they'd like to try differently next time. Use these sessions to celebrate small victories and set new goals for future interactions.

Role-playing is more than just a playful exercise; it's a gateway to deeper understanding and improved communication. Through these rehearsals, you build skills that translate into everyday life, preparing you for whatever challenges come your way. It's about finding ways to connect, understand, and support each other despite disagreements.

Integrating role-playing into your relationship encourages proactive problem-solving and fosters an environment where both partners feel heard. By consistently engaging in these exercises, you'll notice an improvement in addressing conflicts outside the role-play setting. You'll appreciate each other's perspectives more, leading to more harmonious interactions.

As you continue exploring role-playing scenarios, tailor them to fit your unique relationship dynamics. Consider the specific challenges you face and create scenarios reflecting these situations. Personalizing role-play exercises makes them more relevant and impactful, providing insights directly applicable to daily life.

Over time, role-playing will become an integral part of your conflict resolution strategy as a couple. It transforms disagreements from obstacles into opportunities for growth and connection, enhancing both partners' ability to navigate challenges with empathy and understanding.

Incorporating role-playing into your relationship toolkit is an investment in its long-term health and happiness. It encourages open communication, fosters trust, and strengthens your bond—ensuring that they're met with grace and resilience even when conflicts arise.

Mindful Communication Techniques

Let's pretend you are sitting across from your partner, the world around you fading into the background as you focus solely on the moment you share. This is the essence of mindfulness in communication, where each word, gesture, and pause holds significance. At its core, mindfulness is about being present—truly present—in every interaction, ensuring that your mind doesn't wander to the past or future but stays anchored in the now. This approach enhances clarity and deepens your connection with your partner. By practicing mindful listening, you allow yourself to absorb words and emotions, creating a space where understanding flourishes. It's about catching the subtle shifts in tone and body language that often go unnoticed, transforming ordinary conversations into profound exchanges. Pair this with focused breathing during discussions, and you'll be better equipped to handle whatever comes your way. When tension arises, a few deep breaths can center you, allowing for more thoughtful responses instead of reactive ones.

To weave mindfulness into your daily life, consider integrating specific exercises into your routine. Mindful dialogue sessions are a great place to start. Set aside a dedicated time each day to engage in conversation without distractions. Turn off your phone, close your laptop, and pay attention to your partner. These sessions are about more than just talking; they're about connecting on a deeper level and exploring thoughts and feelings without judgment. Practice focusing on the present conversation during these dialogues rather than rehearsing what you'll say next. Another effective exercise is breath awareness. Before engaging in potentially stressful discussions, take a moment to focus on your breath. Inhale deeply, hold for a few seconds, then exhale slowly. This simple act calms your mind and body, preparing you to engage constructively.

The impact of mindfulness on communication is profound. By cultivating enhanced focus and attention, you become attuned to your partner's needs and emotions, reducing the likelihood of misunderstandings. You're not just hearing words; you understand their essence and respond with empathy and insight. This attentiveness fosters an environment where both partners feel respected and valued, paving the way for more meaningful connections. Moreover, mindfulness reduces emotional reactivity by promoting a calm state of mind. When you're grounded in the present moment, it's harder for emotions to hijack your responses. Instead of reacting impulsively to a perceived slight or criticism, you can respond thoughtfully, fostering trust and openness.

Intend to make mindfulness a consistent part of your daily life. Each morning, take a moment to reflect on how you'd like to approach conversations that day. You may want to listen more actively or respond with greater patience. Whatever it is, setting an intention helps guide your interactions toward mindful engagement. For those seeking additional support, consider using mindfulness apps for guided practice. These apps offer exercises tailored to enhance your awareness and focus, making incorporating mindfulness into your daily routine easier. They provide structured practices that can be done anytime, at home or on the go.

Mindfulness is not about perfection but about progress. It's about showing up with intention and openness, ready to engage with your partner meaningfully. By embracing these techniques, you create a relationship where communication thrives—where words are exchanged, understood, and cherished.

Throughout this chapter, we've explored various techniques to enhance communication through mindfulness. Each method offers unique benefits that contribute to building stronger connections with those around us. As you continue reading this book, remember that implementing these practices takes time and effort—but the rewards are well worth it.

By adopting mindful communication techniques into your daily routine, you'll experience deeper connections with your partner while fostering an environment where love flourishes naturally without effort or strain—simply by being present together in each moment shared between you both today!

Expressing Appreciation

Think about the last time you felt truly appreciated by someone. It could be a simple thank-you note or a heartfelt acknowledgment of something you did. That warm feeling you experienced is the power of appreciation in action. In relationships, expressing gratitude is a cornerstone for building strong emotional connections. It's about recognizing and valuing each other's efforts, big or small, and can significantly enhance the positive vibes between partners. Gratitude is the glue that holds relationships together, fostering a sense of belonging and emotional security. When you take the time to acknowledge your partner's actions and qualities, you create an atmosphere of mutual respect and admiration. This gratitude doesn't just improve daily interactions. It boosts overall satisfaction by showing that you notice and value each other's contributions to the partnership.

To bring more appreciation into your relationship, try adding specific activities into your routine. One simple exercise is the "Daily gratitude notes." Jot down something you appreciate about your partner each day. It could be as small as making coffee or as significant as their unwavering support during tough times. Leave these notes where your partner will find them—a bathroom mirror or inside their work bag. Another idea is the "Appreciation jar." Place a jar in a visible spot at home, and regularly add notes expressing gratitude for things your partner has done. Over time, this jar will fill with positive affirmations, serving as a tangible reminder of the love and appreciation you share.

Another delightful tradition is the "Weekly appreciation dinner." Take one night a week to enjoy a meal together where you openly express what you appreciate about each other. It doesn't have to be fancy; the thoughts and words count. During this dinner, share specific instances from the week where you felt grateful for each other's actions or qualities. This ritual strengthens your bond and provides a dedicated space for positivity amidst life's chaos.

Consistent expressions of appreciation can profoundly transform your relationship dynamics. Regular appreciation exercises increase positive interactions, fostering a more supportive and loving environment. When both partners feel valued and recognized, it naturally strengthens emotional bonds, making the relationship more resilient to challenges. This practice encourages a cycle of positivity, where expressing gratitude becomes second nature, deepening the connection between you and your partner.

To make expressions of appreciation even more special, get creative with showing gratitude. Personalized thank-you cards are a heartfelt way to express appreciation. Craft a card by hand or online, and fill it with specific reasons why you're grateful for your partner. The personal touch adds a layer of sincerity that generic cards can't match. Additionally, consider sharing appreciation through creative arts or crafts. Consider writing a poem or creating art inspired by your partner's kindness or support. These creative expressions are unique and personal, making them even more meaningful.

As you engage in these exercises, remember that the goal is not just to say thank you but to cultivate an ongoing culture of appreciation in your relationship. It's about recognizing the little things that often go unnoticed and celebrating each other's presence in your lives. Through regular practice, you'll find that appreciation becomes integral to how you interact, enriching your connection and fostering a deeper understanding.

In wrapping up this chapter on practical exercises for lasting change, it's clear that small actions like expressing appreciation can significantly impact your relationship. By integrating these practices into your daily life, you're paving the way for a partnership built on trust, respect, and genuine affection. Moving to the next chapter, we'll explore how these foundational practices set the stage for even deeper emotional intimacy and connection. You'll discover new ways to nurture your relationship, ensuring it continues to grow and thrive.

Chapter Eight

Build Resilience in Relationships

Resilience is the Foundation of Lasting Relationships

Imagine, if you will, a solitary tree standing steadfast amid the wrath of a relentless storm, its roots anchored deep in the nurturing embrace of the soil, gripping tenaciously to the earth with unwavering strength. Such is the embodiment of resilience in relationships. It is the critical capacity to withstand life's unyielding tempests together as partners, bending with the wind yet steadfastly refusing to break. In this profound context, resilience signifies the ability to not only endure but also bounce back from life's myriad challenges, emerging from the storm scarred, perhaps, but undeniably stronger and more intimately connected. This forms the backbone of enduring partnerships, paving the way for couples to navigate through the precipitating difficulties of life without losing sight of the connection that binds them together. Cultivating a resilient mindset empowers couples to view challenges not as insurmountable mountains of obstacles but as transformative opportunities for mutual growth.

The journey towards resilience begins with the elements of emotional support and a true understanding of one another. These are the cornerstones of a strong relationship. When partners engage in active, empathetic listening—when they genuinely hear each other, offering empathy and validation—it creates a sanctuary for vulnerability to blossom. Furthermore, shared values and common goals act as an unwavering compass, guiding the couple's voyage through tumultuous seas and ensuring that they remain harmoniously aligned in their collective journey. Effective communication strategies cannot be overstated; they provide both partners to feel heard, validated, and valued, creating a steady framework that can weather life's inevitable ups and downs.

Building resilience in a relationship involves the thoughtful establishment of a "resilience routine," a devoted time when couples regularly check-in. These important conversations go beyond the routine activities of daily life; they delve into emotional well-being and the deeper connections that unite the couple. Engaging in resilience-building activities like embarking on team challenges can further cement your bond. Whether it involves the collaborative pursuit of completing a challenging home project or participating in a friendly yet competitive game, these shared experiences foster a sense of teamwork, camaraderie, and trust. They serve as vivid reminders that you are on this journey together, capable of overcoming any obstacle life presents.

Resilience in relationships is not merely about surviving through adversity but about thriving and flourishing despite it. It significantly reduces the weight and impact of stressors, allowing you to confront challenges with renewed confidence and composed assurance. Emotional security is fortified and nurtured as trust deepens, creating an atmosphere in which both partners know that their relationship will remain a steadfast and secure harbor, even when the fiercest of storms strike. This stability brings long-term satisfaction, as both individuals feel genuinely safe and lavishly supported within the relationship. With this in mind, it becomes clear that you are not simply building a relationship but constructing a formidable partnership designed to withstand the inexorable test of time.

Resilience

Take a moment to reflect on all the different past challenges you've bravely faced together as a couple. Write down the vivid recollections of these circumstances and engage in thoughtful discussions with your partner. How did you both handle these moments of adversity? What intrinsic strengths did you discover in each other during these trying times? This reflective exercise is intended to help you genuinely appreciate your collective resilience while at the same time identifying possible areas for growth and improvement.

Resilience is not a fixed endpoint but a perpetually evolving journey filled with commitment and nurturing, especially when the road becomes challenging. By steadfastly focusing on emotional support, shared values, and effective communication, you are laying the essential groundwork for a resilient and enduring partnership. As you continue to build resilience together, always remember that every challenge you overcome serves to fortify your bond, preparing you ever more thoroughly for whatever lies ahead on this shared journey.

Adapt to Life's Changes Together

Change is a constant companion in every relationship. Whether it's a sudden career transition, a surprise relocation, or the exciting yet daunting prospect of starting a family, life keeps us on our toes. These shifts can catch you off guard if you're unprepared, leaving both partners scrambling to find balance. The ability to adapt is crucial. It's about learning to dance in the rain rather than waiting for the storm to pass. As you navigate these inevitable changes, remember that adaptability is your best friend. Embrace it with open arms, and you'll find that even the most challenging transitions become manageable.

Regularly revisiting and reassessing shared goals is one of the most effective strategies for adapting to change. As circumstances evolve, so should your aspirations and plans. Sit down together and discuss what you want individually and as a couple. This ongoing dialogue keeps you aligned and ensures that you're moving in the same direction. Open discussions about expectations and roles are equally important. Talk about who will handle what tasks when life throws a curveball your way. Flexibility in decision-making processes is key here; be willing to adjust plans as needed without getting stuck in rigid thinking.

Support networks can help couples adapt to change. Involvement in community groups or clubs can provide a sense of belonging and a source of encouragement when times get tough. These connections offer fresh perspectives and shared experiences that remind you you're not alone in facing life's ups and downs. Seeking guidance from mentors or counselors can also be invaluable. They bring expertise and objectivity, helping you navigate tricky situations with wisdom and clarity. Sometimes, an outside perspective is all it takes to see things in a new light.

Adaptability brings many benefits, chief among them being a strengthened partnership through joint problem-solving. When you tackle challenges together, you develop a sense of camaraderie that deepens your bond. You're no longer just two individuals facing adversity; you're a team working towards common goals. This collaboration helps grow enhanced creativity in finding solutions as you brainstorm ideas and explore new approaches together. Openness to change encourages innovative thinking, allowing you to discover possibilities you might not have considered otherwise.

Adaptability isn't just about surviving change; it's about thriving amid it. As you learn to roll with the punches, you'll find that your relationship grows more resilient with each challenge overcome. Flexibility and openness create a foundation of trust and security, assuring you both can weather any storm together. The ability to embrace change with grace and confidence is a testament to your love's strength. By adapting to life's changes together, you create a partnership that stands the test of time, ready to face whatever comes next with courage and resilience.

Change is inevitable, but with adaptability on your side, it's far from insurmountable. Embrace these moments as opportunities for growth, both individually and as partners. Let change be the catalyst that propels you forward into a brighter future together.

Emotional Flexibility Enables Bouncing Back from Setbacks

Think of emotional flexibility as a mental yoga class, where you learn to stretch your emotional responses to fit the situation at hand. It's about adjusting how you react, not just going on autopilot. Emotional flexibility means changing your emotional lens based on what's happening around you. Instead of getting stuck in one way of thinking, you can see things from different angles, which is vital when life throws those curveballs. Embracing change as a natural part of life helps you adapt better when things are unplanned. This skill is like having a mental tool ready to be used whenever life decides to test you.

To develop emotional flexibility, try incorporating mindfulness into your daily routine. Mindfulness practices, like deep breathing or meditation, help you regulate your emotions by keeping you present. When you're mindful, you're less likely to react impulsively. This calm state allows you to choose your response rather than just reacting. Another helpful practice is cognitive reframing. This involves changing the way you look at a situation. For instance, if a disagreement arises, view it as a chance to understand your partner better instead of seeing it as a fight. Reframing shifts your perspective and helps you manage emotions more effectively.

Being emotionally flexible enhances resilience by allowing you to recover faster from conflicts. When disagreements happen, instead of dwelling on them, you can move on more quickly. This agility creates emotional balance and stability within the relationship. You won't find yourself stuck in endless arguments because you can adapt and adjust your approach. This capacity to bounce back keeps the relationship dynamic and prevents stagnation.

Maintaining emotional flexibility has numerous benefits for your relationship. It increases your ability to manage stress because you're not fixating on one way of handling things. You're open to trying different approaches, which reduces pressure. Enhanced empathy and understanding naturally follow when you're emotionally flexible. You're more attuned to your partner's needs because you're not stuck in your own perspective. This leads to a healthier, more harmonious relationship where both partners feel heard and valued.

Imagine a scenario where financial stress hits hard. Instead of spiraling into anxiety and tension, emotional flexibility lets you approach the issue with a calm mind. You work together to find solutions rather than blaming each other. This reduces stress and fosters teamwork.

Incorporating these practices into your life can lead to a profound shift in handling challenges together. Mindfulness and reframing equip you to face setbacks with grace and composure. As you become more emotionally flexible, you'll notice that conflicts lessen in intensity and duration.

The impact of emotional flexibility extends beyond overcoming setbacks. It transforms how you engage with each other daily. When you're open to seeing things differently, you're more likely to approach disagreements with curiosity rather than defensiveness. This openness creates an environment where growth and connection thrive.

In a constantly changing world, being able to adjust emotionally is like having a secret superpower. It empowers you to face challenges head-on without fear or resistance. Emotional flexibility isn't just about surviving but thriving in adversity.

When both partners embrace this mindset, the relationship becomes a source of strength and support, ready to tackle whatever comes its way. This adaptability ensures that love remains vibrant and resilient over time.

Sustain Intimacy During Stressful Times

With all its unpredictable twists, life can sometimes feel like a relentless storm, threatening the foundation of intimacy between partners. Financial pressures, for instance, can seep into your relationship like an insidious fog. Bills stack up, unexpected expenses arise, and money becomes a constant source of tension before you know it. Health-related concerns, too, can cast a long shadow over your connection. These challenges can create emotional and physical distance, whether it's a chronic illness or a sudden injury. The stress of dealing with health issues can lead to exhaustion and frustration, making it difficult to maintain intimacy. In these moments, when the world's weight feels heavy on your shoulders, preserving intimacy requires deliberate effort.

One effective way to nurture closeness during trying times is by scheduling quality time for connection-focused activities. Think of it as an oasis amid chaos—a dedicated time to reconnect without distractions. It doesn't have to be elaborate. A simple evening walk, a shared meal without screens, or even a quiet morning coffee together can work wonders. These moments foster connection and remind you of the love beyond life's challenges. Regularly expressing affection and appreciation is another crucial practice. A gentle touch on the shoulder, a loving note on the kitchen counter, or a heartfelt "thank you" for small acts of kindness can keep the flame bright. These gestures affirm your bond and reassure your partner of your commitment.

Practicing vulnerability through open dialogue is vital for maintaining intimacy under stress. When life's pressures mount, retreating behind walls of silence or frustration is easy. But opening up about what's weighing on your mind can bring you closer. Share your fears and anxieties with your partner, allowing them to support you. Vulnerable conversations create a safe space where both partners feel heard and understood. This openness fosters emotional intimacy and strengthens your connection.

Communication plays a pivotal role in sustaining intimacy during stressful times. Sharing stressors with each other is essential. Talking about what's bothering you lightens the load and transforms individual burdens into shared challenges. Seeking mutual support is equally important. Lean on each other for strength and encouragement, knowing that you're in it together. Active listening is key here—genuinely hearing and understanding each other's needs builds trust and ensures both partners feel validated.

The benefits of sustained intimacy during stress are significant. A strong emotional connection acts as a buffer against life's storms, providing comfort and stability. When you maintain closeness, you're better equipped to handle stressors together. Increased mutual support and cooperation naturally follow as you work as a team to overcome challenges. This collaboration fosters resilience within your relationship, bringing grace and unity in times of adversity.

Think of intimacy as a garden that needs tending, especially during difficult seasons. Regularly watering it with quality time, affection, and open communication keeps it vibrant and flourishing. Even when life's storms rage around you, this garden remains a sanctuary where love thrives despite the chaos.

When stress threatens to pull you apart, remember that maintaining intimacy is not just about grand gestures but about the small, consistent efforts you make every day. These efforts nurture a bond that withstands the test of time and emerges stronger on the other side.

As you go through stressful times together, let intimacy be the anchor that keeps you grounded—a reminder that love is a powerful force capable of weathering any storm.

Growth-Oriented Communication Practices

When we delve into growth-oriented communication, we explore the idea of using every interaction to foster positive transformation and learning within a relationship. It goes beyond simple exchanges, encouraging mutual support of personal and relational aspirations. It's like weaving a tapestry where each thread adds depth and color. Imagine those intimate conversations where dreams about the future unfold - these aren't mere dialogues but seeds for growth. Such exchanges lay the groundwork for a relationship that does more than survive; it flourishes. Growth-oriented communication, therefore, signals a joint commitment to individual and collective evolution, crafting a dynamic where every dialogue can propel both parties toward becoming better versions of themselves.

One particularly beneficial approach to this communication style is regularly incorporating goal-setting discussions. Envision cozy mornings or tranquil evenings where you both sit, perhaps with a cup of tea or coffee, discussing your visions for the next year or even five years. These discussions are more than just target-setting sessions; they are opportunities to bring your paths together, ensuring your goals are aligned. Reflective dialogues also hold great significance. Taking moments to evaluate your progress and openly discussing what is and isn't working can be invaluable. Such conversations develop a sense of accountability and foster a shared understanding of purpose, firmly establishing your commitment to grow together.

The effects of incorporating growth-oriented communication in a relationship can be deeply transformative. As growth becomes a focus, so does the motivation to tackle and overcome challenges that come your way. You transform into partners in progress, offering support and encouragement through setbacks while celebrating achievements together. This collective effort fortifies your bond as you strive towards common objectives and dreams. It's no longer a matter of mere coexistence; you become a team collaboratively constructing a shared future. The joy and fulfillment of witnessing each other's growth bring an intense sense of pride and satisfaction in the relationship.

Embracing a growth mindset is fundamentally crucial in this process. This mindset accepts that every experience contains lessons that contribute to learning and improvement, including the challenging ones. With this outlook, you become receptive to new experiences and ideas, diminishing the fear of failure as it morphs into a springboard for success. This open-mindedness nurtures adaptability and resilience—qualities of immense value in any relationship. Through a growth mindset, challenges transform into avenues for learning and connection rather than barriers that create division.

Reflect on how adopting these practices can dramatically reshape your relationship dynamics. Rather than feeling trapped in repetitive disputes or a sense of stagnation, you introduce your interactions with purpose and intent. Each exchange becomes a gateway to discovering new facets of one another, growing closer, and fostering a more robust partnership. Every word shared becomes an involuntary investment in your mutual future, forming a sturdy foundation resilient to unpredictability of life.

As you include growth-oriented communication practices, you may notice a significant enhancement in your interactions. You will grow more attuned to each other's emotions, aspirations, and needs, which enhances your understanding and empathy. This closer connection enables you to face challenges with greater ease while maintaining trust that you both are committed to supporting each other's continued growth.

Let this reflection on growth-oriented communication serve as a vital piece of the larger puzzle. It's about establishing an atmosphere where love persists and thrives through the tides of change and adversity. In the upcoming chapter, we will delve into the essence of trust, the adhesive holding every element together, granting the stability essential for lasting love. Join us next as we explore the intricacies of building trust and nurturing a relationship through authenticity, sincerity, and vulnerability.

Chapter Nine

Embrace Inclusivity and Diverse Relationships

Communication Strategies for Non-Traditional Relationships

It's a family gathering, and you are surrounded by the comforting aroma of home-cooked meals. The cheerful laughter fills the air as you introduce your partner to curious relatives. In this moment, you embody a unique courage and resilience, navigating a path beyond the traditional concept of couples. The family members, with their warm and welcoming gazes, may be accustomed to the conventional.

Still, your presence and your relationships fill them with wonder and intrigue. This scenario underscores the unique and often challenging path of those in non-traditional relationships—relationships that bravely extend beyond the confines of conventional norms to explore new dimensions of love and companionship.

These diverse relationships, each with its unique beauty and richness, can take many forms and configurations. Non-traditional relationships might include loving polyamorous connections, where love beautifully extends beyond the conventional pair, creating an intricate tapestry of romance and emotional support amongst multiple partners. Then there are blended families, crafted when individuals from different backgrounds merge their lives into one harmonious unit, rich with cultural and personal diversity. In addition, co-parenting arrangements exist, forming partnerships focused on collaboratively raising children with care and intention, even when the romantic ties between the co-parents have gracefully concluded. Recognizing these varied and vibrant structures enlightens our understanding, challenging societal norms and broadening our interpretations of love, commitment, and family in today's world.

In non-traditional relationships, open, honest, and ongoing communication is not just important; it's crucial. It's like an intricate tapestry that weaves your relationship's diverse desires, needs, and expectations together. At its core lies establishing clear boundaries and agreements crafted with love and respect to honor everyone's needs. This process is akin to charting a detailed roadmap, guiding your shared journey, and ensuring everyone is aware and aligned with their roles and expectations.

This roadmap isn't static; it evolves as the relationship grows and changes. Open and honest dialogues, the cornerstone of this evolution, are vital for allowing each relationship member to authenticate themselves. It's a space carved out with care where everyone feels safe and encouraged to voice their thoughts, hopes, and fears. This isn't merely about talking—it's about genuinely being heard and understood, a fundamental need for any relationship, and even more so for those lovingly dwelling in non-traditional spaces. These dialogues reassure everyone that their voice matters, fostering a sense of security and trust.

Transparency and trust are not just important in non-traditional relationships; they're the key to sustaining and nurturing the health and balance of these relationships. Consider incorporating regular trust-building exercises and delightful practices that provide opportunities to connect on a deeper level. Engage in weekly reflections, sharing insights into what went well and what areas might benefit from additional care and attention. These exercises reinforce your connection and ensure that everyone remains aligned. Open discussions about each person's expectations of the relationship can provide clarity and consensus, skillfully preventing miscommunications that might otherwise fester into resentment or conflict. By fostering an environment of open honesty, you create a culture of safety where each partner feels protected and encouraged to share their vulnerabilities without the looming fear of judgment or rejection.

Embracing a variety of relationship structures is not just beneficial; it's transformative. It delivers a treasure trove of invaluable benefits, enriching personal growth and understanding for all involved. One profound impact is the boosting of emotional intelligence. By navigating intricate emotional landscapes, you'll develop heightened empathy, patience, and understanding. Not only does this unlock a more profound appreciation for differing perspectives, but it also broadens your concept of love and commitment beyond the standardized societal frameworks. Engaging in such varied experiences challenges preconceived notions. It opens your heart and mind to a vast realm of human connection and possibility that may previously have gone unexplored.

Relationship

Take a moment to delve into the intricate dynamics of your own relationships. Reflect carefully on the habits you form in communication, the boundaries you establish, and the areas where growth could flourish. Pose contemplative questions to yourself: How effectively do we communicate our needs, thoughts, and expectations? What steps can I take to polish and enhance our relationship's transparency and trust levels? Document your reflections and discuss them openly with your partner(s). This heartfelt exercise uncovers strengths and identifies areas ripe for nurturing, ultimately fostering deeper connections and mutual understanding.

By embracing and exploring the diverse, intricate web of non-traditional relationships, you open doors not only to personal enrichment and fulfillment but also to creating a more inclusive, understanding society that celebrates the boundless spectrum of love in all its many beautiful forms.

Inclusivity in Relationship Dynamics

Inclusivity may initially appear as a contemporary catchphrase in relationships, particularly those underpinned by a deep connection and mutual respect. Yet, it genuinely holds significant weight and importance. Picture inclusivity as a grand dinner table adorned with various dishes, where each person's unique culinary creation is celebrated with genuine enthusiasm and appreciation. This scenario mirrors the essence of Inclusivity within a relationship—honoring diverse identities, backgrounds, and life experiences that each partner brings into the partnership. Imagine your relationship as a magnificent mosaic in which each tile contributes to an intricate and breathtaking masterpiece, no matter how distinct in shape, size, or color. Crafting such a mosaic goes beyond merely fitting disparate pieces together; it revolves around valuing these individual elements and perceiving how each enriches the narrative, infusing it with vibrancy and depth. When embracing Inclusivity entails a conscious effort to acknowledge these differences, be they rooted in diverse cultural backgrounds, personal histories, or varying life experiences, and use them as a source of strength.

Implementing practical and thoughtful strategies to nurture inclusivity ensures that every partner is enveloped in appreciation and dignity during every interaction. Initiating with simple steps, one can incorporate inclusive language practices into daily dialogues, knowing fully the power of language. This initiative can appear as subtle changes, such as consistently asking for preferred pronouns or bypassing assumptions tethered to conventional gender roles. Wielded with care, language shapes perceptions and constructs reality, making it essential for the vocabulary we choose to reflect respect and genuine acceptance of all involved. Furthermore, inclusivity transcends the realm of mere dialogue—it invites a rich tapestry of diverse viewpoints into all decision-making processes. Let it become second nature to actively solicit and embrace the perspectives of each partner when navigating decisions, be they monumental or minute. This practice honors individual autonomy and contributions and imbues the decision-making process with many insights and innovative ideas, elevating shared outcomes.

Yet, achieving inclusivity within relationships entails navigating its fair share of challenges. Chief among these is the unconscious biases that frequently lurk beneath the surface, subtly shaping our interactions and perceptions without our conscious realization. These ingrained biases instill resistance towards ideas and experiences that deviate from our preconceived assumptions. Addressing this facet demands an unwavering commitment to self-awareness and growth, starting with acknowledging their presence and deliberately seeking to counteract their influence. Establishing safe spaces that foster open dialogue is crucial for surmounting these obstacles. Cultivate an atmosphere conducive to honest conversations on biases and their potential impact on the relationship, ensuring each voice is heard and wholeheartedly respected, even amidst differing viewpoints.

Inclusivity's influence on a relationship's overall health is significant and far-reaching. When partners feel sincerely valued and recognized for their unique traits and strengths, it fosters a deep, abiding connection grounded in mutual respect and compassionate understanding. This shift naturally enhances empathy, as inclusivity invites partners to view the world through each other's eyes. Such a transformative perspective broadens the horizons for appreciating different lived experiences and viewpoints, ultimately fortifying the resilience of the relationship. During moments of conflict or emotional strain, this resilience provides a vital buffer, enabling the relationship to weather challenges more adeptly and emerge stronger and rejuvenated on the other side.

Embracing inclusivity in its entirety transforms relationships into thriving ecosystems where diversity is wholeheartedly celebrated, not just passively tolerated. It grants relationships the freedom to transcend traditional boundaries, venturing into uncharted territories of love and partnership that might have otherwise remained unexplored. Recognizing each partner's distinct contributions fosters an environment ripe for love to prosper in its myriad expressions, unburdened by societal constraints or stereotypical expectations.

Inclusivity, while immensely beneficial to the relationship, also catalyzes personal growth within the partnership's delicate paradigm. As you delve into diverse perspectives and traverse a broad spectrum of experiences, your comprehension of the world flourishes, nurturing your emotional intelligence and cultivating a well-rounded and adaptable character. This evolution extends beyond the confines of the relationship, enriching other dimensions of life by encouraging a mindset open to new experiences and adaptable to ever-evolving circumstances.

Incorporating such practices into your relational dynamic demands thoughtful intention and steadfast dedication but offers unparalleled rewards that elevate both individual and collective well-being. Inclusivity transcends mere acknowledgment of differences; it calls for celebrating these distinctions as indispensable components that render your relationship uniquely exquisite and enviable.

As you read this chapter, which is dedicated to the essence of inclusivity in relationships, take a moment to reflect on how these principles resonate with your own experiences and interactions. Identify areas where inclusivity could be nurtured further and explore innovative approaches to cultivating a setting where all partners feel seen, heard, and cherished. Through intentional language choices and inclusive decision-making practices, each meticulous effort directed towards inclusivity plays a pivotal role in fostering a more interconnected and compassionate partnership.

By embracing the full spectrum of inclusivity and implementing its core tenets—recognizing the diversity of identities, valuing unique contributions, confronting and overcoming biases, and nurturing mutual respect—you lay an enduring foundation for a relationship that not only thrives on diversity but also flourishes in the boundless and profound depths of love.

Address Cultural Differences in Communication

There's a warmly lit table, its polished surface gleaming under a soft glow. Beside you, your partner gently places a dish before you, aromatic with unfamiliar spices that dance in the air. Each dish whispers tales from a land you are yet to explore, with flavors that promise journeys through a history distinct and different from your own. This experience is like navigating cultural differences in any relationship, where every exchange is imbued with the vivid colors of diverse backgrounds. Cultural diversity is a prism, refracting interactions through its many facets, sometimes in subtle ways that remain unnoticed until one has learned to pay attention.

For instance, the realm of non-verbal communication holds a myriad of secrets that shift significantly from one culture to another. A simple nod is a gesture of agreement. Still, in some cultures, it's reserved for a slightly different context, potentially leading to confusion if assumptions are made. Eye contact represents another facet—while it stands for honesty and assertiveness in certain societies, it might appear impolite or aggressive in others. Recognizing such variations becomes crucial in paving the way for smoother paths in communication, allowing the depths of a relationship to be explored with respect and understanding.

Emotional expressions weave yet another layer of complexity into this tapestry. Cultures may encourage the open expression of feelings, bold and effervescent. In contrast, others might teach restraint, grace under pressure, and composure as virtues. This knowledge can be a key to unlocking the true meanings behind your partner's expressions and reactions, preventing potential misinterpretations from sowing seeds of discord. Recognizing that, for some, a calm demeanor during heated debates might not signify a lack of empathy. Still, a deeply held cultural value allows for navigating conflicts with greater care and sensitivity.

Bridging these cultural divisions is akin to building a bridge over a vast river, connecting two worlds once apart. Engaging in cultural exchange activities can be a first step in constructing this bridge. Dive into each other's world through the vibrance of cultural festivals, the artistry of preparing traditional meals together, or the wisdom shared in stories of historical events that have shaped your partner's heritage. These shared endeavors build understanding and cement companionship as you create shared memories from these new explorations.

Exploration can be furthered by learning about each other's intrinsic cultural norms and practices. Ask questions sincerely, listen with attentive curiosity, and walk into every conversation ready to be amazed by your partner's unique background. Such steps communicate respect and demonstrate your willingness to embrace the diversity they bring into your shared life. By shaking off assumptions forged by stereotypes, you give yourself permission to see your partner's identity in all its rich complexity.

Cultural sensitivity plays a crucial role in harmonious communication. Active listening becomes a valuable ally here. When your partner shares narratives woven from the threads of their culture, give them space to unravel these tapestries fully. Listen with eyes that seek understanding and minds that hold judgment at bay. This dedicated attention reaffirms your appreciation for their honesty and determination to immerse deeply into their world.

At times, perspectives can be clouded by assumptions rooted in stereotypes. Yet, each individual's cultural story is uniquely theirs, interwoven with threads beyond mere ethnicity or nationality. Embracing this multifaceted complexity while shedding preconceived labels fosters an environment wherein partners can express their authentic selves without fear.

Cultural diversity presents unparalleled richness, infusing relationships with vibrancy and depth. It transforms perspectives, challenging preconceived notions, and invites you to experience the world with fresh eyes. Such diverse interactions enhance your empathy, encouraging you to glimpse the world through various cultural lenses. Your ability to adapt and thrive within diverse societies strengthens as you adeptly navigate the subtleties of intercultural communications.

Diversified cultures extend an invitation to personal and relational growth, encouraging explorations into uncharted territories and broadening preconceived perceptions about love, commitment, and partnership dynamics. When embraced together, these challenges nurture resilience and appreciation for diversity's inherent beauty.

There develops a richness woven into life as you integrate vibrant cultural elements into the tapestry of your relationship. A treasure trove awaits, bustling with experiences otherwise unexplored—novel traditions, exquisite cuisine, stories that captivate—all waiting to be celebrated and cherished.

As you engage in the realm of cultural communication with your partner, remember that each encounter is an opportunity for connection and growth. Approach these experiences with an open heart and curious mind, and let them guide you towards an improved understanding of each other and the ever-expanding world you share.

Embracing cultural diversity within your partnership is like unlocking doors to endless possibilities. This realm enriches your relationship, illuminating your life's path with unimagined wonders.

Keep the Spark Alive in Long-Distance Love

Long-distance relationships can feel like a never-ending waiting game, testing your patience and resolve to the fullest extent. You and your partner might reside in different cities, countries, or even continents, separated not just by the physical distance but sometimes by cultural and temporal oceans that may seem almost impossible to reach across. This geographical separation undeniably presents a unique set of challenges that couples with the luxury of frequent face-to-face interaction might never encounter. Among these obstacles, the limited physical presence is undoubtedly one of the most glaring. The comforting embrace that follows a harrowing day or the reassuring gaze exchanged in silence across a crowded room are irreplaceable gestures that speak volumes without needing words. The absence of these small yet incredibly significant gestures can, at times, amplify the emotional distance, making it seem even more substantial than the miles separating you.

Another formidable challenge is the disparity in time zones, often transforming the simple act of scheduling a phone call into a logistical puzzle akin to orchestrating a symphony. Picture yourself bursting with excitement, eager to relay a moment of triumph or seek solace after a challenging day, only to remember that your partner is sound asleep on the other side of the world. These time differences can foster feelings of isolation and estrangement, as though you and your partner exist in parallel universes, living within different time realities. However, despite these challenges, after persistent effort and unwavering commitment, numerous couples manage to sustain their love, allowing it to survive and thrive against all odds.

The key to success lies in maintaining a resilient and strong connection, even when you are miles apart. If harnessed with intention and creativity, technology emerges as your most formidable ally. Planning regular virtual date nights becomes crucial. During these moments, you can share the experience of watching a movie, transit worlds through online games, or engage in heart-to-heart conversations over a meal, replicating the cozy evenings you yearn for. Video calls and messaging apps serve as lifelines, offering the opportunity to divulge in daily experiences and mundane happenings, infusing life with little yet significant shared moments. This consistency emerges as a cornerstone, vital in bridging the metaphysical gap and ensuring the emotional bond remains steadfast and robust.

On the other hand, creativity has an undeniably significant role in nurturing long-distance love. Sending surprise care packages with personal tokens, cherished mementos, or heartfelt handwritten notes can make your partner feel treasured and incessantly remembered. Simple gestures like sharing playlists or books, potentially birthing a virtual book club, fostering engagement, and allowing discussions and reflections on various thoughts and feelings. These creative and thoughtful approaches inject fun and excitement into the relationship, converting potentially monotonous weeks into periods of anticipation and joy.

Another pivotal strategy is setting future goals, a beacon of hope and direction amidst uncertain waters. Having tangible plans to look forward to together provides a palpable sense of purpose and alignment. Discussing timelines about in-person visits or exploring potential relocation paths ensures both are striving towards a shared and coveted future. Conversations surrounding shared aspirations and life objectives gain paramount importance. Whether it's deliberating on the next visit, contemplating career transitions, or envisioning cohabitation in dream locales, these discussions are critical to maintaining alignment and motivation.

In the intricate dance of long-distance relationships, communication morphs into the immutable cornerstone that holds everything together. It transcends logistical exchanges or superficial daily updates; it embodies the sharing of dreams, unveiling of fears, celebration of victories, and staunch support during trying times. When physical presence is sparse and scattered, words transform into powerful and imaginative bridges that connect hearts across formidable distances. Openly sharing your feelings and engaging in active listening foster trust and understanding, both crucial when miles span between you.

As you wade through this chapter dedicated to the nuances of long-distance love, it is imperative to remember that every relationship is uniquely its own. What resonates profoundly with one couple might not elicit the same connection in another. The essential task is to discern what resonates with both of you and remain agile as circumstances evolve. Although long-distance relationships may test your endurance and creative faculties, they also afford opportunities for personal growth and profound emotional connection.

As we draw this chapter on embracing inclusivity and appreciating diverse relationship dynamics to a close, remember that every bond is fraught with its distinctive challenges and rewards. By recognizing and cherishing these differences, a solid foundation emerges upon which love can triumphantly thrive. In our next chapter, we build resilience together, addressing life's turbulent ebbs and flows with grace and fortitude. Stay tuned for insights purposed at transforming challenges into opportunities for personal growth, further deepening your connection.

Chapter Ten

Sustain Growth and Connection

Set Relationship Goals Together

You and your partner, united in a shared vision, are seated at a cozy table with a blank canvas before you. This canvas is not just a space for painting but a platform for collaboratively creating the vibrant future of your relationship. Setting relationship goals is a journey of unity and collaboration. It's about dreaming together, projecting a shared future, and drawing a detailed map of how you will arrive. This process isn't just about grand dreams and aligning your visions to foster ongoing growth. Envision long-term relationship visioning as a guiding roadmap to trace where you desire to stand in the far-reaching spans of five or even ten years. It's about cementing a home, nurturing a family soulfully, or exploring the world's vastness together. These expansive dreams act as anchors, giving your relationship a sense of direction and purpose.

While setting these lofty, far-off goals forms essential pillars of your shared journey, it's crucial not to sideline the often-overlooked short-term aspirations. These smaller, immediate goals are not to be underestimated. They lay the groundwork for enduring commitment, offering refinement and enhancing relational dynamics sooner. Small goals could manifest as dedicating intentional time for weekly date nights or as tangible improvements in communication skills. They are the building blocks that sustain momentum and cultivate confidence, essential for tackling grander, more formidable challenges as a united front.

Constructing actionable goals as partners necessitates moving beyond idle conversations. A well-defined game plan crystallizes ambitions into achievable actions. The SMART goals framework—**S**pecific, **M**easurable, **A**chievable, **R**elevant, and **T**ime-bound—is a proven method to transform aspirations into concrete strategies. Envision sitting down together to craft a vision board overflowing with compelling images, timeless quotes, and salient reminders of your shared goals. This vivid display becomes a constant daily beacon, illuminating your aspirations and keeping both sails hoisted on your journey.

Accountability emerges as a cornerstone in the journey toward realizing these goals. One side of the coin is identifying and acknowledging intentions, but the commitment to following through is equally vital. Regular check-ins are essential touchpoints where progress can be evaluated, victories celebrated, and plans adjusted as necessary. Imagine it as a supportive nudge, ensuring that neither partner loses track of the shared goals being pursued. Establishing accountability partnerships within the fabric of your relationship becomes a source of profound strength, transforming you into one another's steadfast supporters and buoying spirits during setbacks.

Goal-setting has a profound impact on relationship dynamics. The collaboration required in pursuing shared goals fosters robust teamwork, the same as rowing a boat in perfect synchronicity. Both partners paddle harmoniously toward their destination, motivation equally propelled by shared enthusiasm. This collective effort enhances focus and facilitates overcoming obstacles along the way. Each goal achieved becomes a stepping stone that deepens understanding as partners cultivate a deeper appreciation for each other's strengths, championing support through weaknesses, thus reinforcing a partnership enriched by every triumph.

Shared goals inherently advocate mutual understanding, underscored by the necessity for open dialogue and the grace of compromise. Expressing desires, negotiating needs, and finding common ground is an ongoing exercise in empathy and patience, unfailingly strengthening the relational bond. It underscores the truth that it's not merely about arriving at the finish line but the evolving, rewarding journey of growth and connection accompanying the partnership.

Vision Board Creation

Devote a leisurely afternoon to the rewarding exercise of creating your vision board together. Gather a variety of magazines, printed materials, scissors, glue, and a large poster board. Start this engaging activity by individually sharing your personal goals and dreams, then collaboratively blending them into harmonious shared aspirations. As you cut and collect images, words, or phrases that resonate with the future you both envision, arrange them meaningfully on the board. Once displayed prominently in your shared living space, the completed vision board is an enduring prompt for the exciting adventures and milestones you are striving toward.

Incorporating goal-setting into your relationship is more than a pursuit of dreams; it is a potent mechanism for bolstering growth and sustaining connection. By weaving shared objectives into your relational narrative, you nurture a partnership where both individuals feel invaluable and deeply invested in sculpting a fulfilling future. It transforms the dynamics of your relationship into an ever-evolving journey—a thrilling expedition studded with challenges and discovery.

As you chart goals together, embrace flexibility as an indispensable virtue. Life flows unpredictably and plans frequently demand adaptability. Welcome these diversions as enriching growth opportunities rather than viewing them merely as setbacks. Maintain an adaptable mindset open to adjusting goals while steadfastly focusing on what remains genuinely significant—the enduring bond and love shared between you.

Setting relationship goals extends beyond a mere exercise; it embodies a sustained pledge to each other's happiness and enrichment. It embodies grand dreaming coupled with concrete actions that ground those dreams in reality. So, claim your metaphorical blank canvas and embark on painting the magnificent tapestry of your joint future—it promises to be nothing short of breathtaking!

Continuous Learning and Adaptation

Your relationship is a living, breathing entity that thrives on nourishment from love and affection and continuous growth and learning. Relationships, much like any living thing, demand care and adaptability. This idea of lifelong learning in relationships isn't confined to academic pursuits. Instead, it involves engaging in activities that foster personal and mutual growth. By embracing continuous learning, you and your partner can develop resilience, shielding your relationship from life's inevitable storms. Consider engaging in joint educational activities, whether it's a cooking class that brings out your competitive spirit or a language course that opens doors to new cultures together. These shared experiences become the threads that weave a richer tapestry of connection, fostering adaptability as you learn to navigate unfamiliar territories together.

Change is often seen as a disruptor, yet it holds immense potential as a catalyst for growth when approached with an open heart and mind. Embracing change as a growth opportunity means welcoming the unexpected with curiosity rather than resistance. It involves seeing every shift, whether a career change or moving to a new city, as a chance to expand your horizons individually and as a couple. This mindset transforms challenges into stepping stones, allowing you to build a partnership that survives and thrives amid the shifting tides of life.

To integrate learning into your relationship, consider practical methods that encourage regular engagement with new ideas. Enrolling in workshops or classes together can be a fun way to deepen your bond while acquiring new skills. It could be anything from a dance class that gets your heart racing to a seminar on financial planning that prepares you for the future. These activities provide structured opportunities for growth, where you both can learn side by side, supporting each other through the process.

Another effective strategy is to read and discuss relationship books, opening the floor for conversations about different perspectives and ideas. Choose books that challenge your current thinking or offer insights into areas you want to explore together. As you discuss what you've read, you'll enhance your understanding of each other and develop communication skills crucial for navigating complex discussions.

Adaptability isn't just about adjusting to change; it's about thriving in it. Being open to new ideas and experiences allows your relationship to evolve in ways you might never have imagined. Practicing flexibility in roles and responsibilities within the relationship can prevent stagnation and foster a dynamic partnership. One week, you take on more household chores while your partner focuses on a demanding project at work, and the next week, the roles switch. This kind of fluidity ensures that both partners feel supported and valued.

Encouraging creative problem-solving is another way to enhance adaptability. When faced with challenges, approach them with an open mind, considering unconventional solutions that might not be immediately obvious. This mindset encourages innovation and collaboration, turning potential roadblocks into opportunities for connection and growth.

A relationship grounded in continuous learning is dynamic and fulfilling, offering countless benefits that enhance personal and relational growth. Engaging in lifelong learning fosters a deeper understanding of each other's evolving needs and desires, creating a partnership rich with mutual respect and admiration. The more you learn, the better equipped you are to navigate challenges, transforming them into moments of growth rather than sources of conflict.

Additionally, this commitment to learning enhances your ability to adapt to changes within the relationship. As you grow individually, your relationship naturally evolves, requiring adjustments in connecting and communicating. By embracing this evolution as part of the learning process, you create a resilient partnership capable of weathering any storm.

Learning

Set aside an evening each month for an "educational date night," where you both choose a topic you're interested in exploring together. It could be anything from watching a documentary on a subject you've always been curious about to attending a local lecture or event. Afterward, discuss what you've learned and how it might apply to your relationship or personal life. This exercise enriches your knowledge and deepens your connection through shared exploration.

Using these strategies, your relationship creates an environment where learning becomes second nature—a natural part of your everyday interactions. As you continue to engage in continuous learning and embrace change as an opportunity for growth, you'll find that your relationship becomes more adaptable, resilient, and fulfilling.

Build a Supportive Partnership Community

Creating a supportive community around your relationship can be like discovering a hidden treasure chest. Imagine having friends who understand exactly what you're going through, offering advice and a shoulder to lean on. Emotional and practical peer support becomes invaluable, reassuring you that you're not alone in your experiences. Shared experiences and learning opportunities arise naturally within such circles, where you can exchange stories, ideas, and resources that benefit your relationship. This external network acts like an extended family, ready to celebrate your highs and help you navigate the lows.

To connect with others sharing similar relationship goals, consider exploring various avenues. Joining couples' groups or clubs offers an excellent way to meet like-minded individuals. These gatherings often involve activities both partners enjoy, ranging from book clubs to hiking groups. They provide a fun, engaging environment where friendships blossom naturally. If face-to-face meetings aren't feasible, don't underestimate the power of the digital world. Online forums and social media communities serve as virtual hubs where couples can gather, share advice, and bond over common experiences. Participating in these platforms allows for flexible interaction, accommodating busy schedules yet providing valuable support.

Another valuable resource for relationship growth is seeking guidance from mentors and role models. Think of these individuals as guiding stars, illuminating the path with wisdom gained from experience. Engaging with established couples and relationship experts offers insights into navigating challenges you might face. These mentors can provide personalized advice rooted in years of experience, helping you avoid pitfalls and reinforcing your strengths. Similarly, relationship coaches offer tailored strategies to enhance your partnership. Their professional input can catalyze breakthroughs, helping you see issues from fresh perspectives.

The impact of community involvement on relationships is profound. Access to diverse perspectives and advice equips you with a rich arsenal of strategies for tackling various challenges. It broadens your understanding of relationship dynamics and introduces innovative solutions you might not have considered. Moreover, a supportive community fosters a sense of belonging and shared purpose. It transforms your relationship into part of something more significant than yourselves—a network of love and support that strengthens your connection.

For those wondering how to start building this community, it begins with openness and initiative. Reach out to friends with similar values or interests; they might know of existing groups worth joining. Attending local events or workshops designed for couples can also be a great way to meet others prioritizing their relationships. These gatherings create opportunities for natural connections, leading to lasting friendships that enrich your lives individually and together.

In addition to traditional methods, technology's role in fostering connections cannot be overstated. Online platforms like Facebook groups or dedicated apps for couples offer spaces where you can engage with others virtually while reaping the benefits of communal support. These digital communities often feature discussions on various relationship-related topics—everything from communication tips to fun date ideas—creating an interactive resource pool at your fingertips.

Building a supportive partnership community isn't just about seeking help but also offering support. By sharing your experiences and insights with others facing similar challenges, you contribute positively to the collective wisdom within these networks. This reciprocal exchange fosters a sense of camaraderie where everyone benefits from each other's knowledge and experiences.

An essential aspect of nurturing this community involves recognizing its dynamic nature—it grows and evolves alongside your relationship. As you encounter different stages or challenges in life together, lean on this network for guidance while remaining open to offering support when needed.

The value of having a supportive partnership community becomes evident when facing life's inevitable ups and downs together. Whether celebrating milestones or navigating hardships, knowing there's an entire network standing by, ready to lend encouragement, makes all the difference.

Ultimately, cultivating such communities enriches your relationship and your personal growth journey as individuals committed to nurturing love in all its forms.

Celebrate Milestones and Progress

Celebrating milestones in your relationship is like adding vibrant colors to a painting, each brushstroke bringing more life and detail to the masterpiece you're creating together. These celebrations are not just for the big, apparent moments like anniversaries or birthdays but also for the more minor, everyday victories that often go unnoticed. Recognizing major and minor accomplishments reinforces positive behaviors and acknowledges the effort you both put into nurturing your relationship. It's about creating a culture of appreciation where achievements, no matter how small, are cherished and celebrated. This mindset fosters an environment where love and gratitude flourish, strengthening your bond with each passing day.

When it comes to commemorating these milestones, creativity plays a key role. Organizing anniversary or milestone parties offers an opportunity to gather loved ones and share the joy of your relationship's journey. If parties aren't your thing, consider creating a "relationship scrapbook" filled with memories, photos, and mementos that capture the essence of your shared experiences. This tangible collection becomes a cherished keepsake that you can revisit time and time again. Planning special trips or experiences lets you step out of the ordinary and into adventures that create lasting memories. Whether it's a weekend getaway or a once-in-a-lifetime vacation, these experiences reinforce your bond and add depth to your relationship.

Reflection is integral to celebration, offering a chance to pause and reflect on how far you've come. Journaling reflections on achievements provides insight into your growth as a couple, highlighting the lessons learned along the way. Discussing these lessons together reinforces what you've achieved and sets the stage for future goals. It's a chance to recognize patterns, celebrate strengths, and identify areas where you can continue to grow. This reflective practice deepens your understanding of each other, creating a strong foundation for ongoing improvement.

Regularly celebrating progress offers numerous benefits that ripple through your relationship. One such benefit is increased relationship satisfaction, as acknowledging achievements fosters a sense of fulfillment and pride in what you've built together. These celebrations strengthen emotional connections, providing moments of closeness that remind you why you chose each other in the first place. They remind you of the love and commitment that underpin your relationship, motivating you to continue striving for growth.

The act of celebration itself becomes a catalyst for motivation, inspiring you to set new goals and pursue them enthusiastically. Acknowledging what you've achieved fuels a desire to reach even greater heights together. This ongoing cycle of celebration and reflection nurtures an environment where both partners feel valued and appreciated for their contributions to the relationship.

Milestone Celebration Ideas

Try setting aside time each month to celebrate your progress, whether over a homemade dinner or a leisurely walk in the park. Use this time to share what you appreciate about each other's efforts and discuss any significant milestones you've reached. You could also create a "celebration jar" where you jot down accomplishments on paper throughout the month. At the end of each month, take turns reading these aloud and reflecting on the journey so far.

As we conclude this chapter on sustaining growth and connection, remember that celebrating milestones is more than just marking time—it's about honoring the path you've walked together and the dreams you're yet to realize. By fostering an attitude of gratitude and celebration, you nurture a relationship that thrives on positivity and mutual support. This foundation prepares you for whatever challenges lie ahead, reinforcing your bond with every step forward.

Conclusion

Thank you for taking this journey with me through "Couples Communication Code." Our time together has been about unraveling those frustrating communication knots and discovering new ways to connect more deeply with your partner.

Throughout this book, we've touched on some vital core themes for any thriving relationship. We've explored empathy, the ability to truly understand and share your partner's feelings, and emotional intelligence, which helps you navigate your own emotions and those of your partner. Conflict resolution was another key focus, offering you tools to transform disputes into opportunities for growth. We also looked at customizing your communication style to suit your needs, ensuring that your unique ways of expressing love and concern are acknowledged and respected.

My vision has always been to empower you to enhance your communication skills, fostering deeper connections and lasting love. I want you to feel equipped to end those cycles of fights, rebuild trust, and talk honestly without triggering each other. The dream is for you to have conflict-free conversations that lead to a more profound connection with your partner.

Remember the importance of active listening and empathy as you reflect on what we've covered. These are your tools for genuinely hearing and understanding your partner. Breaking negative patterns is crucial, too, as it opens the door to healthier communication and a more supportive relationship environment. And in this digital age, finding the right balance between digital and in-person communication is essential to maintaining intimacy.

We've discussed practical strategies together, such as exercises for active listening and empathy-building. We've also discussed role-playing for conflict resolution and the importance of nurturing intimacy even during stressful times. These aren't just theoretical ideas but actionable daily steps to improve your relationship.

Now, it's your turn. I encourage you to implement these strategies and exercises. Engage actively with the concepts we've discussed. Make them a part of your daily life. Remember, your progress so far is a testament to your commitment and effort. Change doesn't happen overnight, but you can transform your relationship with continued dedication.

Continuous growth is not just a goal but a journey. As your relationship evolves, so should your communication approaches. Stay open to learning and adapting. This flexibility will foster sustained growth and connection, allowing you and your partner to navigate life's changes together. The journey of growth is ongoing, and it's what keeps our relationships vibrant and alive.

Consider engaging with a supportive community. Whether you join a couples' group, participate in online forums, or simply share your journey with friends who understand, these communities can offer valuable insights and encouragement. They can also be a source of strength as you work to improve your relationship. Don't hesitate to share your progress and challenges with them; their support can be invaluable.

I want to express my deepest gratitude for embarking on this journey. Your willingness to explore and improve your communication speaks volumes about your commitment to your relationship. It's been an honor to guide you through this process, and I want to remind you that your active participation and commitment are crucial to its success.

Remember, effective communication is not just a tool but a powerful force that can transform your relationship. It can turn challenges into opportunities for deeper understanding and love. As you move forward, keep this positive message in mind. You have the tools and motivation to foster conflict-free, empathetic, and meaningful conversations. Embrace the journey ahead with optimism and love, knowing that you're building a more fulfilling and lasting relationship with each step.

For more people to benefit from the information in this book, they need your help. If this book was informative and of use to you, please leave an honest review to help others recognize this resource.

References

- *Empathy and Human Relationships, NYC.* (n.d.). https://integrative-psych.org/resources/empathy-and-human-relationships#:~:text=Understanding%20and%20Validation%3A%20Empathy%20helps,and%20care%20about%20their%20experiences

- *EI Overview: The four Domains and twelve Competencies – Daniel Goleman Emotional Intelligence Courses.* (n.d.). https://danielgolemanemotionalintelligence.com/ei-overview-the-four-domains-and-twelve-competencies/

- Cuncic, A., MA. (2024, February 12). *7 Active listening techniques for better communication.* Verywell Mind. https://www.verywellmind.com/what-is-active-listening-3024343

- Duckworth, C. (2024, July 12). *The Double Empathy Problem: Bridging Communication Gaps with Emotional AI — Emotional AI Analytics - Valence Vibrations.* Emotional AI Analytics - Valence Vibrations. https://www.valencevibrations.com/blog/the-double-empathy-problem#:~:text=Seek%20common%20ground%3A%20Focus%20on,gap%20and%20building%20stronger%20rela tionships

- LeBlanc, P. (2017, August 8). *Negative Communication patterns: How to reverse them*. Compass Counseling. https://compasscounseling.org/how-to-reverse-these-negative-communication-patterns/

- Counseling, T. a. S. C. (2024, April 1). *Understanding emotional triggers and building healthy relationships | Therapy in St. Petersburg, FL*. Sunshine City Counseling. https://www.sunshinecitycounseling.com/blog/emotional-triggers-and-relationship-issues-in-therapy

- Paul, M. (2016, August 16). *Moving from Blame to Accountability - The Systems Thinker*. The Systems Thinker. https://thesystemsthinker.com/moving-from-blame-to-accountability/

- Editorial Team. (2024, November 3). *27 Key tips to Overcome Conflict Avoidance in Relationships*. Marriage Advice - Expert Marriage Tips & Advice. https://www.marriage.com/advice/relationship/how-to-overcome-conflict-avoidance/

- Green, R. (2023, May 26). *What your conflict resolution style says about you and is it healthy?* Verywell Mind. https://www.verywellmind.com/5-conflict-resolution-styles-is-yours-healthy-7503353

- Lisitsa, E. (2020, December 3). *Manage Conflict: Repair and De-Escalate*. The Gottman Institute. https://www.gottman.com/blog/manage-conflict-repair-and-de-escalate/

- *7 Gottman Techniques for Navigating Life Tran-*

sitions in Relationships - Ascension Counseling & Therapy. (n.d.). Ascension Counseling & Therapy. https://ascensioncounseling.com/7-gottman-techniques-for-navigating-life-transitions-in-relationships

- Lpccmhc, K. R. M. (2022, March 10). It isn't comfortable, but it fosters communication and connection. *Psychology Today*. https://www.psychologytoday.com/us/blog/happy-healthy-relationships/202203/the-importance-of-vulnerability-in-healthy-relationships#:~:text=Why%20is%20vulnerability%20important%3F,you%20on%20a%20deeper%20level

- *Building trust in dialogue.* (2025, March 22). https://udayton.edu/blogs/dialoguezone/22-10-06-building-trust-in-dialogue.php

- Team, A. (2024, January 22). *How to create an emotionally safe space.* American Press Institute. https://americanpressinstitute.org/how-to-create-an-emotionally-safe-space/

- Cohen, R. (2021, May 4). *5 Ultimate Vulnerability Exercises - Seaside Counseling Center.* Seaside Counseling Center. https://seasidecounselingcenter.com/5-ultimate-vulnerability-exercises/

- Nadeem, R., & Nadeem, R. (2024, April 14). *Dating and relationships in the digital age.* Pew Research Center. https://www.pewresearch.org/internet/2020/05/08/dating-and-relationships-in-the-digital-age/

- Marriagefamily. (2024, June 24). *Digital detox for cou-*

ples: Reconnecting without screens. Marriage and Family Services. https://www.marriagefamilyservices.com/post/digital-detox-for-couples/

- Team, Z. (2024, January 6). *8 Communication Exercises in Long-Distance Relationships | Zencare*. The Couch: A Therapy & Mental Wellness Blog. https://blog.zencare.co/long-distance-relationship-communication/

- User, A. (2025, March 4). *Ground rules for couples in the digital Age - Symmetry Counseling*. Symmetry Counseling. https://symmetrycounseling.com/uncategorized/ground-rules-for-couples-in-the-digital-age/

- Growth, C. F. (2024). Gottman Communication Assessment. *Counseling | Therapy*. https://thecenterforgrowth.com/tips/gottman-communication-assessment

- *How communication styles in relationships affect your connection*. (2024, November 21). Elevate Counseling + Wellness. https://www.elevatecounseling.com/blog/how-communication-styles-in-relationships-affect-your-connection/

- *What are the most effective strategies for communicating with people who have different communication styles?* (2023, September 14). https://www.linkedin.com/advice/1/what-most-effective-strategies-communicating

- Greenberg, M., PhD. (2019, August 12). If you're married or dating, these tools will help you overcome negative cycles. *Psychology Today*. https://www.psychologytoday.com/us/blog/the-mindful-s

elf-express/201908/6-powerful-communication-tools-for-satisfying-relationships

- Carpenter, D. (2024, January 24). *How to develop empathy in relationships*. Verywell Mind. https://www.verywellmind.com/how-to-develop-empathy-in-relationships-1717547

- Seid, L. (2023, March 24). *Five tips for building mindful communication*. Marriage Advice - Expert Marriage Tips & Advice. https://www.marriage.com/advice/communication/mindful-communication/

- Lewandowski, G. W., Jr PhD. (2023, October 31). Make each other feel heard, and cope together. *Psychology Today*. https://www.psychologytoday.com/us/blog/the-psychology-of-relationships/202310/7-ways-to-make-your-relationship-more-resilient

- Banks, D. (2024, March 3). *Understanding & promoting psychological flexibility in marriage*. Marriage Advice - Expert Marriage Tips & Advice. https://www.marriage.com/advice/marriage-fitness/psychological-flexibility/

- Koehler, J., PhD. (2024, June 7). Transforming love through continuous learning and mutual growth. *Psychology Today*. https://www.psychologytoday.com/us/blog/beyond-school-walls/202406/how-a-growth-mindset-can-enhance-romantic-relationships#:~:text=Partners%20with%20a%20growth%20mindset,partners%20feel%20heard%20and%20valued

- Inclusive Therapy Group. (n.d.). *Effective communication in polyamorous relationships*. https://inclusivetherapygroup.c

om/blog/communication-in-polyamorous-relationships

- Hill, H., & Hill, H. (2024, December 26). *Cultural Impact on Modern Relationships: A deep dive.* Start My Wellness, Ferndale, MI. https://startmywellness.com/2024/06/cultural-differences-shape-relationships/

- Manson, M. (2023, February 8). How to survive a long distance relationship. *Mark Manson.* https://markmanson.net/long-distance-relationships

- Lmft, M. H. (2024, May 7). *The Power of Goal Setting in Relationships: A Step-by-Step Guide for Couples.* Holding Hope Marriage and Family Therapy. https://holdinghopemft.com/the-power-of-goal-setting-in-relationships-a-step-by-step-guide-for-couples/#:~:text=Goal%20setting%20in%20relationships%20refers,navigating%20life%20as%20a%20team

- *4 reasons lifelong learning can transform your 2025.* (2024, December 17). UC News. https://www.uc.edu/news/articles/2022/01/4-reasons-to-become-a-lifelong-learner-for-the-new-year.html

- Casaba, M. G. (2024, July 22). Building a support network: the value of community and mentorship. *Advancing The Seed, Inc.* https://www.advancetheseed.org/blog/building-a-support-network-the-value-of-community-and-mentorship

- Pace, R. (2024, March 28). *15 relationship milestones that are worth celebrating.* Marriage Advice - Expert Marriage Tips &

Advice. https://www.marriage.com/advice/relationship/relationship-milestones-that-are-worth-celebrating/

- Doctor, D. (2023, June 24). *Relationship conflict resolution miss date doctor*. Miss Date Doctor® - Relationship Coaching London Couples Therapy London Dating Coach London Marriage Counselling London. https://relationshipsmdd.com/relationship-conflict-resolution-miss-date-doctor/

- Greg. (2024, November 30). *Love in Action: How empathy Can Transform your relationships*. Valiant Couples Therapy and Consulting. https://www.valiantcouplestherapy.com/post/love-in-action-how-empathy-can-transform-your-relationships

- Vanremmerdenl. (2024, July 8). Tech Timeout: A digital detox guide. *Fourtees*. https://www.fourtees-brand.com/post/tech-timeout-a-digital-detox-guide

www.ingramcontent.com/pod-product-compliance
Lightning Source LLC
Chambersburg PA
CBHW070629030426
42337CB00020B/3961